Praise for *The Kindness Principle*

This is a wonderful book, which anyone who cares about children and young people will find compelling. It challenges so much of the current orthodoxy about macho 'no excuses' school cultures and has lessons for us all about relationships and the impact of fear, humiliation and shame on young people.

Fiona Millar, education journalist, *The Guardian*

Dave Whitaker's book is a game changer. It's a behaviour management book for teachers, support staff and school leaders written by someone who actually does it for a living whilst carrying themselves with credibility and integrity. This is no self-help book. It's a call to loving arms.

Hywel Roberts, teacher, writer, speaker and humorist

The Kindness Principle captures decades of Dave Whitaker's thinking and experience in an inclusive and practical book.

Stephen Tierney, Chair, Headteachers' Roundtable,
and author of *Educating with Purpose*

How can anyone object to kindness? Particularly when it comes to children. There are so many elements of this book that resonate: the need for adults to be their authentic selves with lived values, the power of recognition and intrinsic motivation, the value of play and co-constructed rules, the rigour of flexible consistency, the effect of seeing attention-seeking behaviour as attention-needing behaviour, and the fundamental problems of using fear and sanctions to control children and demand respect.

Fran Morgan, founder of Square Peg

Dave's work is so much more than kindness: it is relational, successful and replicable. And what he shares in *The Kindness Principle* is unconditionally excellent and seriously useful.

Paul Dix, behaviour specialist, WhenTheAdultsChange.com

The Kindness Principle is a book I want to read again and again. Since reading the book, my interactions with dysregulated pupils have improved – and my belief that kindness and relationships should be at the heart of every school has been strengthened.

Simon Kidwell, Head Teacher, Hartford Manor Primary School and Nursery

Dave Whitaker's *The Kindness Principle* is a book that speaks up for children – and it is a really good read. It sheds light on the rituals, routines and habits of the school system and shares current research findings and practical advice to enable teachers and others in school to consider how best to give children every opportunity to succeed and to enjoy their education.

Mick Waters, Professor of Education, University of Wolverhampton

The Kindness Principle is a wonderfully crafted book that reminds us of the value and impact of kindness and authentic leadership in schools. Dave poses a series of provocations, encouraging the reader to consider the systems and leadership behaviours evident in their schools – and challenges them to rethink them. A must-read for anyone who works with children and young people.

Kate Davies, CEO, White Woods Primary Academy Trust

In *The Kindness Principle* Dave takes us on a '25-year learning walk' with a coherent philosophy of education, a characteristic humility and a sound grounding in neuroscience. Whether it's practical insight into micro-structures and de-escalation, new knowledge on neurochemicals needed for learning, or the emotional resonances of tricky situations recounted with students and staff, the book shares a lot of powerful learning for educators and leaders at all levels.

Kiran Gill, CEO, The Difference

The Kindness Principle is a must-read book for enlightened educators which provides a practical guide to relationships-led practice. Between these covers, you'll find everything you need in order to become a school where teachers love to teach, learners love to learn and where curiosity and empathy turn adversity into opportunity.

Dr Pooky Knightsmith, expert on child and adolescent mental health

In *The Kindness Principle*, Dave provides invaluable insights into the essential ingredients that shape successful behaviour management strategies in schools. I have known Dave for a decade and I believe that he is one of the wisest and most highly respected voices in this field.

Jon Chaloner, CEO, GLF Schools, Vice Chair, Headteachers' Roundtable

Perhaps one of the greatest mistakes we can make in education is to see the virtue of kindness as somehow irrelevant or, worse still, weak. What Dave Whitaker's beautiful book shows us is that the opposite is true.

Ben Walden, Director, Contender Charlie

The
Kindness
Principle

*Making relational behaviour
management work in schools*

Dave Whitaker

ındependent
thinking press

First published by

Independent Thinking Press
Crown Buildings, Bancyfelin, Carmarthen, Wales, SA33 5ND, UK
www.independentthinkingpress.com

and

Independent Thinking Press
PO Box 2223, Williston, VT 05495, USA
www.crownhousepublishing.com

Independent Thinking Press is an imprint of Crown House Publishing Ltd.

First published 2021.

Edited by Ian Gilbert.

Page 15, social discipline window: adapted from Ted Wachtel and Paul McCold, Restorative Justice in *Everyday
Life in Restorative Justice and Civil Society* © H. Strang and J. Braithwaite (eds), Cambridge University Press.
Reproduced with permission of the Licensor through PLSclear. Page 80, circle of influence: adapted from David
Moore (2011) The circle of intimacy [video] (21 November). Available at: https://www.youtube.com/watch?v=0A-
iTNk0Cj4 © Crown 2007. Page 94, pattern of stress model: all rights reserved © 2007–2021 Bruce D. Perry.
Pages 96–97, sensitising patterns diagrams: all rights reserved © 2007–2021 Bruce D. Perry.

Independent Thinking Press has no responsibility for the persistence or accuracy of URLs for external or third-party websites
referred to in this publication, and does not guarantee that any content on such websites is, or will remain, accurate or appropriate.

Quotes from Ofsted and Department for Education documents used in this publication have been approved under an Open
Government Licence. Please see: http://www.nationalarchives.gov.uk/doc/open-government-licence/version/3/.

British Library Cataloguing-in-Publication Data

A catalogue entry for this book is available from the British Library.

Print ISBN 978-178135385-1
Mobi ISBN 978-178135386-8
ePub ISBN 978-178135387-5
ePDF ISBN 978-178135388-2

LCCN 2021931059

Printed and bound in the UK by
Gomer Press, Llandysul, Ceredigion

This is for Josie – she was a principal, she had strong principles and she was kind. I wish she were here to read this book.

Foreword

I feel very privileged to have been invited to write this foreword. Dave's book is one of those rare gems: a really useful education book. It is a book that will take courage to read – and even more courage to apply the approaches advocated within it.

I am not a teacher but, having talked to schools as a neurobiologist and paediatric neurologist for over three decades, it is my experience that almost all of the hundreds of teachers whom I have had the privilege to meet are motivated by a single desire: to do their best for the children and young people under their care. It is to that high ideal that this book gives fuel and substance. We sit at a time when education is being split into two halves: old-style Victorian teaching methods and modern methodologies based on compassion and understanding. As an observer it is hard, at the moment, to see how any commonality can be found between the two. This book lays out ways of thinking about education which any teacher can engage with and then apply to themselves and the children and young people in their care.

To each and every teacher reading this I would ask you to think carefully about the principles and discussions in this book. Ask yourself, are the premises sensible? Do they contain that one essential: common sense? I think that you will likely say, 'Well, yes. This all seems very sensible.' I would agree. There is a depth of understanding in this book of how to successfully lead children and young people into that most important of things: self-motivated learning. It has always been my belief that an excellent education is one that produces exactly this.

The deeper principle that is also explicit in this book is probably the most significant one – if you, as a teacher, can develop and own the core principles that are set out here, then you will experience that most wonderful of things: a really enjoyable and often profound life. If you are experiencing that then your pupils will experience the wonder of having a great teacher.

Andrew Curran

Acknowledgements

I have to say thanks to many people who have helped me to be in a position where I can say that I have actually written a book. That probably needs to begin with my 'persuader', Ian Gilbert. The encouragement was subtle but effective, even if it did take years. Thanks also to Dr Andrew Curran for not only providing scientific inspiration but for being kind enough to write the book's foreword.

It goes without saying that this would not have happened without the support of my family – Mum, Dad, Zoe and Ben – but especially my youngest son, Joe, who was my own personal editor and checker. He spent hours by my side explaining sentence structure and grammar – something that was missing from my own education in the 1980s. He certainly is a credit to modern education but also to his own teachers at Hall Cross Academy in Doncaster.

I have to say a huge thank you to the friends and colleagues who have motivated and inspired me over the years – those teachers who champion the most vulnerable children every day. Verity Watts for keeping me thinking, Hywel Roberts for his enthusiasm and support, Danny Ross and Luke Mitchell for being relational experts and gurus in their own right. The staff, past and present, at Springwell in Barnsley, who are the most committed and passionate educators I could have ever wished to work with. And all those who work in Wellspring schools now, carrying the commitment, resilience and passion of unconditional positive regard with them every day.

More recently, I have reason to thank Kiran Gill and Fran Morgan for their eagerness to make a difference to children's life chances and for their help with the data. Also, Louise Penny from Independent Thinking Press for making my work look good.

Contents

Contents

Introduction:
It must start with kindness

There can be no keener revelation of a society's soul than the way in which it treats its children.

Nelson Mandela[1]

Kindness is defined as the quality of being friendly, generous, and considerate. Affection, gentleness, warmth, concern, and care are words that are associated with kindness. While kindness has a connotation of meaning someone is naive or weak, that is not the case. Being kind often requires courage and strength.

Karyn Hall[2]

Kindness can sometimes be perceived as weakness and, when associated with behaviour management in schools, can be a real conundrum. Is it possible to use kindness in a way that leads to successful behaviour management? How is it possible for a school to have kindness as its basis for relational behaviour management and still have children who show respect, follow the rules and achieve success? It is hard to believe that kindness, as a foundation for behaviour management, could be questioned or doubted – but it is. If we aspire to be relational in our approach to behaviour management, then we must start with kindness. Kindness can mean being tough and fair – exposing frailties and weaknesses but doing it with warmth and compassion. To remain kind in difficult and challenging environments takes courage and strength.

---

1   Address by President Nelson Mandela at the launch of the Nelson Mandela Children's Fund, Pretoria, 8 May 1995. Available at: http://www.mandela.gov.za/mandela_speeches/1995/950508_nmcf.htm.
2   Karyn Hall, The Importance of Kindness, *Psychology Today* (4 December 2017). Available at: https://www.psychologytoday.com/gb/blog/pieces-mind/201712/the-importance-kindness.

We are living in an era of polarised views on managing behaviour. Fast-track school improvement is based on creating compliance at all costs. High levels of strict conformity are seen as a strength in many schools, even if the collateral damage is high exclusions and cohort change. Many schools across the country employ a system based on strict consequences and sanctions. They use this compliance, along with the threat of punishment, to successfully 'control' the behaviour of most of the children in their care. But what do we mean by 'successfully'?

Exclusion[3] is viewed as an acceptable and inevitable consequence of a system in which, without compliance, there is no other option. It is regarded as an unavoidable and tolerable side effect of what are perceived as successful behaviour policies. Strict compliance at all costs is even viewed by some proponents as a positive life lesson that prepares children for adulthood and the 'real world'.

However, surely a behaviour policy should only be viewed as successful if exclusion is not needed? Arguably, if a behaviour policy must rely on the cliff-edge sanction of exclusion, then it is not successfully changing behaviour for the better. If a school permanently excludes a child, then perhaps they are admitting defeat – that they aren't able to manage their behaviour. This is inevitably going to provoke controversy, but the idea should at least be explored and debated. As educators, we should all ask ourselves the question about what successful behaviour management actually is. Permanent exclusion essentially means passing the problem onto someone else. It certainly is not a cure.

Should we, as education professionals, regard schools as successful if they do not do their very best to work with the most challenging and vulnerable children in society? Some children need additional support, guidance and flexibility in their educational journey. Some pupils have specific additional needs that cannot be met in a mainstream environment. Some need to move to specialist settings because it is in their best interests to do so. However, some are excluded because the system is failing them; they are moved from school to school because nobody is repairing the damage and making the adjustments that they need in order to be successful. Schools too often focus on dealing with the symptoms of challenging behaviour,

---

3   At the time of writing, the Department for Education are looking determined to change the term 'exclusion' back to the old and antiquated term 'expulsion'. They are also likely to bring back the term 'suspension' to replace fixed-term exclusion too. This seems like a backwards step and a totally unnecessary change, but one I would like you to note. Either way, all these terms still have an extremely negative connotation that we could do without.

not the causes. There is a small but seemingly ever-increasing cohort of children – if my experience is anything to go by – who are either excluded from education or trapped in a cycle of punishment, which seems to be considered an acceptable consequence of a widely used and highly regarded behaviour strategy. We must ask ourselves whether this is OK.

Behaviour management in schools begins with our choices as adults and our behaviour as professionals. Yes, we can write out our behaviour policy and have the rules, rewards and sanctions clearly displayed on classroom walls, but it is our understanding of, and ability to deal with, relationships that really influences behaviour. We all need to be careful with our choices as education professionals. We can, and do, choose where to work, who to work for and who to work with. This book will explore how kindness, strong relationships and an understanding of behaviours (of both adults and children) can lead to successful and happy schools in which children and adults thrive, struggle, laugh and cry together.

We are constantly influenced by those with whom we work, live and socialise. We all work with, or have worked with, leaders and colleagues who either inspire us or frustrate and infuriate us. We must always be willing to learn and develop by exposing ourselves to new ways of working and thinking. We must be led by our core values but also willing to adapt and change throughout our careers as we gain more experience, knowledge and understanding. In the modern world of fake news and social media, we are exposed to strong opinion and polarised views, more so than ever before. Educational debate, particularly on social media, can be both enlightening and utterly frustrating. We must be willing to listen to and learn from the wise. Wisdom is powerful, but it comes from genuine experience and not just from research and books. Books help, as does data, but there is no substitute for wisdom gained through experience.

After starting my career as a secondary school geography teacher – leading inclusion and special needs – and then moving into headship, executive headship and becoming a National Leader of Education (NLE), I found myself in academy trust leadership. This book is a twenty-five-year 'learning walk' through challenging, urban, disadvantaged primary and secondary schools, pupil referral units (PRUs) and social, emotional and mental health (SEMH) – previously known as behaviour, emotional and social difficulties (BESD) – special schools, as well as academies and free schools, and the teaching, training, outreach, support and leadership that goes with it. It may help you to make those challenging choices and find contentment in your job and organisation. But, whether content or not, behaviour management is never easy. It is a roller coaster of emotions and stress, which causes us to suffer constant highs and lows. It changes from class to class, week to week and year to year. You think you have got it sorted and then an hour later you think you are a failure. It definitely does not become easy – it just gets easier than it was. Working in challenging schools with complex children is both truly rewarding and exceedingly hard work. It relies heavily on your personal resilience, your ability to accept getting things wrong, and your understanding that when it does go wrong, it is not necessarily anyone's fault. It is about trying to do your very best for the children who need you – and never underestimating how powerful that need may be.

In 2018 *The Guardian* published an article about the school where I was lucky enough to be the then executive principal and the way in which we used kindness at the heart of our values and philosophy.[4] Looking back, it seems incredible to think that being kind to children was worthy of making the national news – or any news at all. It is also amazing to think that the article received criticism from some for a style of behaviour management that was considered soft, and that I, as the head, was even considered a danger to the teaching profession because of my relational approach. It did, however, open up a debate which allows us to explore the values associated with managing behaviour. It allows us to consider in detail how we treat children in our care and to ponder what it is we are trying to achieve in our schools.

Although this book draws on some thinking from the worlds of therapy and neuroscience, I must be clear that I am neither a therapist nor a neuroscientist – I am a 'schoolist'. This book is written about schools and for the people who work in them – whoever you may be and whatever role you have.

---

4   Josh Halliday, 'We Batter Them with Kindness': Schools That Reject Super-Strict Values, *The Guardian* (27 February 2018). Available at: https://www.theguardian.com/education/2018/feb/27/schools-discipline-unconditional-positive-regard.

Chapter One

Unconditional positive regard

Don't smile until Christmas?

Before we delve deeper into the behaviour of children in school – the challenges it brings, the emotions it generates and the solutions we need – we should first reflect on the work of Carl Rogers, the author of numerous books focused on the humanistic approach to psychotherapy. Rogers believed that:

> For a person to 'grow', they need an environment that provides them with genuineness (openness and self-disclosure), acceptance (being seen with unconditional positive regard), and empathy (being listened to and understood). Without these, relationships and healthy personalities will not develop as they should, much like a tree will not grow without sunlight and water.[1]

Rogers was an American psychologist who pioneered a person-centred approach to understanding human relationships. His work is widely used in the fields of psychotherapy and counselling but less so in modern education. However, if we look at the following quote, I think you might be able to see why it may be applicable for us:

> The therapist experiences a warm caring for the client – a caring which is not possessive, which demands no personal gratification. It is an atmosphere which simply demonstrates 'I care'; not 'I care for you *if* you behave thus and so.' [...] It involves an acceptance of and a caring for the client as a *separate* person, with permission for him to have his own feelings and experiences, and to find his own meanings in them. To the degree that the therapist can

---

1   Saul McLeod, Carl Rogers, *Simply Psychology* [blog] (5 February 2014). Available at: https://www.simplypsychology.org/carl-rogers.html.

provide this safety-creating climate of unconditional positive regard, significant learning is likely to take place.[2]

If a therapist can do this, then surely a teacher can too?

So, Rogers coined the term 'unconditional positive regard', which can be emotive and generate polarised views and misconceptions. It is being used more and more in schools and can form the starting point for developing values and a relational ethos for working with children. For us, this outlook is the bedrock for developing relational behaviour management. It is a term that, when used in a school context, should make us think about our relationships with children and adults alike. It is often unnecessarily overcomplicated. 'Unconditional positive regard' should be taken in its most simple interpretation, applied to all, and lived on a daily basis. Therefore, let's look at what this means in practice and at how a school can use unconditional positive regard as a method that sets the tone and values for a relational approach, to drive the behaviours of the adults and act as a point of reference and safety for difficult decision making.

- **Genuineness:** Children know when adults are fake. In fact, adults know when other adults are fake. Genuineness in our own actions, decisions and behaviours begins to build an authenticity in relationships that can be used to drive behaviour at all levels. Genuineness builds trust. It champions honesty and transparency. Self-disclosure, as difficult as it may seem, supports the authenticity required to be genuine.

- **Acceptance:** Everyone needs to be and feel part of something. As adults, we know that. Many children struggle to find acceptance in a group, in a school, or even in a family. Unconditional positive regard can provide the foundation for acceptance. The children in your school need to feel accepted and understood. Acceptance allows them to build self-esteem and to trust others. We must not assume that acceptance happens automatically at school, even for the most well-rounded children, with supportive families and happy childhoods. Some schools demand conformity as a prerequisite for acceptance, so this is often a barrier that is difficult to break down for those who struggle to understand their place in school. As adults, with the power to influence

---

2   Carl R. Rogers, *On Becoming a Person: A Therapist's View of Psychotherapy* (Boston, MA, and New York: Houghton Mifflin Company, 1961), pp. 283–284.

acceptance, we must not let our preconceptions of conformity prevent our acceptance. We must be highly aware of children who may be struggling to feel accepted. If we do not spot this, then we are in danger of letting pupils slip through the net. They may develop school-based anxiety or even stop attending. If children stop attending school because they don't feel accepted, it will be very difficult to repair the damage and get them back. This can lead to long-term school refusal, high levels of anxiety and significant problems with transition to the next phase of education.

- **Empathy:** It is important that we do not mistake sympathy for empathy. Sympathy, which is often important, is a feeling of pity or compassion for another person. Yes, this can be invaluable, but empathy is what helps us with unconditional positive regard. Empathy, in this sense, is stronger and allows us to understand another person's feelings and identify with them. Genuine empathy can be challenging, and it's something with which many people struggle. Avoiding pity and putting ourselves in the place of the other person is a much more powerful stance.

- **Self-actualisation:** We must each try to be our ideal self, even if the environment – the school, the conditions in which we work – tries to prevent this. The type of person you wish to be is the person your behaviours should portray. This is where we must again be authentic, and our ideal self must fit our actions. If you are not careful, you can get trapped in a system that does not match your values, does not allow you to express yourself fully and restricts you in being your true self.

The use of unconditional positive regard in a school setting is sometimes misunderstood and, in some cases, used in a negative way to criticise and condemn a school ethos and an approach to behaviour management. Taken without understanding, or without seeing it in practice, it can be interpreted as being soft, ineffective and unproductive. However, the truth is very different. A great way to frame unconditional positive regard is to relate it to your own children, or those of close friends, or your nieces, nephews or grandchildren. You expect them to behave and you challenge and support them to do so. They test you and pull on your emotions. They can make you laugh and cry. They frustrate you and at times even anger you. But you never stop loving them. You give them a fresh start every day, you love them unconditionally and will do everything in your power to give them a happy and successful future. Is that being soft? Is that being ineffective?

Using unconditional positive regard as a starting point in your thinking about behaviour management in school will help you to understand the power of relationships. It becomes an excellent way to examine the importance of adult behaviours, authenticity and a genuine understanding of the children we often struggle with in our classrooms. It allows you to think about the person and the professional you want to be – your ideal self. It is not, and never will be, an excuse. It does not mean low expectations, or having a lack of rigour, or letting children 'get away with it'. It certainly does not mean having cosy cups of tea and chocolate biscuits with pupils, rather than holding them to account. It does not mean that we compromise our standards and allow poor behaviour.

It does, however, mean that we aim to truly understand the children we teach. It means that we, as adults, need to be aware of our own behaviour and the impact this has, not only on the children but on our colleagues too. It also means that we understand that successful behaviour management starts with a set of values and principles that we believe in, and an ethos upon which we can build our policies. Without this belief in what we do, this approach will not work. Relational behaviour management relies on true belief and authenticity, and on every adult working together for the genuine good of the children, whatever they do. That is the hard bit. Being judgemental about children and families is not helpful in forging strong relationships. We often hear – even now – about new teachers being told to be firm and strict: not to smile until Christmas. Well, how about being warm and kind? Working to develop positive relationships from day one, without feeling like you need to be anything but your true self, is vital. This will give you the start to your career that sets the tone for years to come. If you get this wrong, become a nasty teacher and not your true self, then you will turn classes against you. Pupils will not warm to you and that will be the reputation and image you have to live with each day.

The more I can keep a relationship free of judgment and evaluation, the more this will permit the other person to reach the point where he recognizes that the locus of evaluation, the center of responsibility, lies within himself.

Carl Rogers[3]

So, our values take over and steer our behaviours. In an ever-changing, highly pressured education system, we will constantly find ourselves tested.

An example from practice

Faye would arrive at school every morning to be greeted at the front door with smiles and warmth from the staff. She was young and vulnerable. As a ten-year-old she was exposed daily to things that most of us would not hope to experience in a lifetime. Neglect and poverty had been her reality since the day she was born; she knew nothing else. She lived in a constant state of anxiety and hypervigilance, both at home and at school. She was naturally defensive, having spent all her young life living with low-level threat and a constant sense of fear. She had been excluded from mainstream primary school and did not have a secure, safe place or relationship in her life. On arrival at school she struggled with being met with the warm greeting and personal reception that she did not receive anywhere else. When staff welcomed her with a cheery 'Good morning, Faye', she simply replied – under her breath and without looking up – 'Fuck off'. Was this an act of defiance from a naughty child who was looking to make a stance against authority, or was this the response of a lonely and troubled girl who wasn't willing or able to form relationships, because that would mean letting her guard down and risking rejection?

Faye responded like this every morning for over a year. Not once did the staff stop offering a warm greeting to Faye. They did not reject her, and those closest to her would constantly encourage her to stop telling everyone to fuck off. They told her she did not need to push us away, because we all cared about her. Eventually she began to realise that the school community was not going to reject her. She had

---

3   Carl R. Rogers, *On Becoming a Person*, p. 55.

been in many scrapes and incidents that year and yet she had not been excluded like she was in her previous schools. Faye changed her morning greeting to a simple muffled grunt and dropped the aggressive swearing. This continued for some months but eventually the real change came. When greeted with the customary warm welcome from the staff, Faye now responded in her own trusting way with a simple 'Morning, sir' or 'Morning, miss'. Faye had learnt that the welcome she received every day was genuine. It was authentic and caring – if she let her guard down, she would not risk being rejected. Faye said good morning to the staff every day from then on. She left Year 11 with her GCSEs and went to college happily. She still went home every day to neglect and poverty, but school was safe, and the adults genuinely cared. Do not let the term 'unconditional positive regard' scare you. Embrace it and use it.

I was first introduced to unconditional positive regard by the late Josie Thirkell, who was my head teacher when I first worked in special education. She was the executive head teacher of Barnsley PRU and Springwell Community Special School, where she persuaded me to leave mainstream and become her deputy in 2008. She was also the founder and first CEO of Wellspring Academy Trust. Josie was an inspiration then and remains so now – a true mentor and sadly missed, dear friend. I often reflect on how she introduced me to a simple behaviour policy which, as her deputy, I needed my help to instil in a new BESD school and a struggling PRU. The policy was, and remains, very simple: be kind to the children, build relationships, understand them well and support the staff to teach great lessons. Unconditional positive regard was to become our joint mantra for the next five years – and mine for the rest of my career. Yes, we looked at the work of Rogers and at his background in counselling, but that was not our focus.

Simple, influential leadership

Josie was a head teacher but she was also a trained counsellor. She felt that a therapeutic approach was invaluable when supporting vulnerable children and, although she didn't practise as a counsellor, it was a way of working that leant itself to school life and to a relational approach to leadership – I was sold. The focus was simple: compassion, empathy, kindness and fresh starts. She never once accepted anything less than high expectations and high standards of behaviour but insisted that we show the children love no matter what they may have done. She taught me not to get too bogged down in theory, to go with my gut feelings and be true to what I believe in. These wise words have driven me to this day. In fact, as research develops, more books are written, more 'experts' emerge and more gurus impose their expertise on the profession, I will always come back to those wise and genuine words from someone who was a true expert and guru. Experts are made through hard graft, doing the work and spending hour after hour and day after day in schools. Gurus are not created from reading, writing books or blogs, or talking to people – they need to be there on the ground with their sleeves rolled up.

Everyone can look back at their leadership influences and career-defining moments, and this was one of mine. Our challenge was to make sure the school, its staff, the children and their parents all understood and believed in the simplest of values – unconditional positive regard. School improvement, for us, was not about complicated development plans with key performance indicators and success criteria, logged and measured against milestones and resource allocation; it was a list of jobs that needed to be done, and right at the top was developing school culture. We started with unconditional positive regard, explained it to the whole staff and quite simply asked anyone who could not work with us to leave. Luckily, everyone stayed. From that point onwards, every year, in September, I would work with the staff to re-establish the ethos of the school, to share our values and co-construct what we felt were the most important cultural connections we wanted to achieve together. Having done this, I would then make it clear that anyone who did not believe in these values needed to find another job somewhere else. Nobody ever chose to leave.

Try this

- If you are a school leader, consider introducing the idea of unconditional positive regard to your whole staff. Use it as a starting point to discuss, reflect on and co-design your school values. Make sure the concept is not overcomplicated and ask your staff to decide what they think it means before sharing the definition from Carl Rogers. Allow your staff to examine what this concept would look like in practice and suggest how it can be incorporated into school life.

▪ If you are a teacher, consider this concept when working with your most challenging class. Begin to understand the children, their backgrounds and their challenges. Use unconditional positive regard when making decisions or indeed when reflecting on past decisions.

We know that great schools do not need to show an Ofsted outstanding banner on the front gate. Wonderful schools open their doors to visitors and there is pride and warmth in every corridor and classroom. Staff and children are happy, and the community is thriving. Unconditional positive regard is tangible in every interaction. Great schools do not need a badge of honour; they live what they believe and that is what makes them truly outstanding.

Achieving and embedding unconditional positive regard in a school takes commitment and belief. Without belief it just will not happen. It also takes time. The values of a school do not exist just because they are written on a website; they are not established because the staff are told that they must adhere to them. They are created and embedded over time because they are genuine and lived. A values-based culture, from its inception to its embedding, can take between three and five years to build – but it is worth it.

Chapter Two

Creating a culture

Values must be seen, not just written

Adult behaviour must always be the basis of any behaviour policy and its practical implementation in a school. It is the responsibility of all adults to be leaders of values, creating the right ethos and setting the tone of the school every day. Values are lived and should never be just a statement on a website or a list on the classroom walls. When values are lived, a culture is created. All schools will, at some stage, develop a set of values that they proudly print on letter heads, planners and the prospectus. The challenge is to recognise how these values are actually lived out in the school every day. In fact, are we convinced and confident that they are?

Your values, in a person-centred profession like education, should be your fundamental beliefs and therefore drive your behaviour. They should be the guiding principles that steer every relationship and interaction you have, whether that is with a colleague or a child. You are far more likely to be happy if you are successfully living out your values in your everyday life. It is not healthy to work in a system that doesn't align with your own values. Therefore, you must look after yourself as well as provide the best possible place for children to learn. It is up to you to decide what makes the 'best' place for learning and how you can influence that.

Try this

▓ If you are a school leader, invite someone else into your school to tell you what they think your values are. This is a brave move but will ultimately be rewarding. Open your school up to a few (depending on the size of the school) senior colleagues from other schools. Select people who you trust and who understand your school. They should also be confident enough to challenge and question you. Ask them to spend the day in your school, in classrooms, the playground, the dinner hall and staffroom. Ask them one simple question that they will endeavour to answer over the course of the whole day: 'What are the values that you see being lived in this school?' At the end of the day, allow your colleagues to feed back to you and the senior team. You could even invite a few governors. You now truly know the values of your school. Either celebrate them (by putting them on the wall, the website and the letter head) or make a plan to change them.

If you are a teacher, ask a colleague to observe one of your lessons. Do not ask them to comment on the quality of your teaching or the strength of the curriculum. Simply ask them to tell you what they think your values are. Be brave and give it a go. Then decide if you are happy with the feedback, and what you might need to do about it.

As leaders (and we are all leaders in our own classrooms), we must always reflect on how we form relationships, whether in the classroom or across the whole school. Consider how that influences behaviour and, importantly, how our behaviour makes others feel. This is the same for working with children and managing their behaviour. We each have hundreds of personal interactions a day, each one of them influencing our response and our behaviour. If we, as adults, react to the tone, manner and style of another adult's interaction then why would that be different with children? To be clear, it is not any different. Children will respond to you depending on how you present yourself, the tone of your voice, your body language and what you say. Furthermore, they will respond to you depending on how you respond to them. In Chapter Eight we will explore the power of language and how this can influence changes in behaviour. We will also consider how restorative approaches can be used as part of a successful behaviour policy.

Once, when chatting to an experienced and respected colleague with responsibility for school leadership development at a national level, she favourably referred to a head teacher we both knew and complimented him for being 'ruthless'. I questioned her about that term and why she thought that it was a good thing. She had clearly lost sight of what great leadership is and, for some unknown reason, thought that the harshness of 'ruthless' leadership was a trait to celebrate. She associated this leadership style with fast school improvement, high exclusions and, therefore, 'success'. I am not sure I could ever say that being ruthless was also being successful, or could ever be considered a positive leadership skill – even if the school improvement was fast!

The social discipline window

As leaders of adults and of children, we must aim to motivate through appropriate levels of challenge and support. The social discipline window, as shown in the following figure, gives us an insight into how adult behaviour can set the tone for an organisation's approach to relationships and leadership tendencies. It was originally modelled by Ted Wachtel and Paul McCold,[1] adapted from Daniel Glaser's work on dynamics in prisons,[2] and brought to my attention by Mark Finnis. Mark is an Independent Thinking Associate and a highly respected colleague and friend. His work in the field of restorative practice has been significant in my thinking and in the development of culture and values in my schools. This diagram is taken from slides he has used in staff training sessions.[3]

Four ways ...

Challenge ↑	To	With
	Not	For
		Support →

---

1   Ted Wachtel and Paul McCold, Restorative Justice in Everyday Life. In Heather Strang and John Braithwaite (eds), *Restorative Justice and Civil Society* (Cambridge: Cambridge University Press, 2008), pp. 114–129.
2   Daniel Glaser, *The Effectiveness of a Prison and Parole System* (Indianapolis, IN: Bobbs-Merrill, 1969).
3   Which, in turn, is adapted from Wachtel and McCold, Restorative Justice in Everyday Life, p. 124.

The social discipline window, then, impacts on how we work with children and support them to do the right thing. This model clearly shows us that high challenge and high support work in harmony to empower and motivate. Working 'with' someone is far more likely to achieve success than doing it for them, doing it to them or not doing anything at all. Taken as a tool for behaviour management, this model can be powerful, enabling both adults and children to feel responsible for their own actions and aware of their own agency.

Try this

■ If you are a school leader, introduce the social discipline window in staff meetings or senior team meetings – and then use it. Keep referring to it and reflecting on which box you are operating in. Talk about it together. Use it when constructing your school development plan or writing the behaviour policy. Adapt it to help frame your performance management process, using it to help plan professional development and training.

■ If you are a teacher, think about the social discipline window when planning lessons or when interacting with pupils. Look at how you can empower your pupils by designing lessons that achieve the ideal balance of high challenge and high support.

Setting the tone

As I have said, we are all leaders, and leaders make the choices and set the tone. Vic Goddard, head teacher of Passmores Academy in Harlow – a mainstream setting in which he advocates the use of unconditional positive regard – and an Independent Thinking Associate and a leader I respect hugely, refers to adults who 'make the weather'.[4] This really is your job. You are constantly setting the tone with your

---

4   This derives from a quote by Haim Ginott: 'It is my personal approach that creates the climate. It is my daily mood that makes the weather.' Haim G. Ginott, *Teacher and Child: A Book for Parents and Teachers* (New York: Macmillan, 1972), p. 15.

mood and your manner. Whether you are a teacher, leader, or anyone else working in a school, your own behaviour and approach really does influence how children behave and, importantly, how they feel. If you are bright and cheery then it is likely that the children will be too. If you are dark and gloomy then you will see how the children respond with their mood.

As leaders, we have a responsibility to create the right working environment in which everyone can thrive – including ourselves. With that in mind, we need to create a world in which stress is reduced as much as possible. It must be an environment in which adults are respected and supported, in which they are provided with the opportunity to work hard with challenge and support. Get that in place and the rest can follow.

As a leader, your behaviour sets the tone for the whole organisation. School staff work hard and under high levels of pressure. Time is precious and often pressured. We can help prevent the feeling of being overwhelmed by making simple adjustments to how we behave as leaders. The guide on page 18 will help you to focus on your behaviour and therefore impact on the behavioural values of the whole school.[5]

Now look at this in relation to being leaders of children. The following simple guidelines can set the tone for your approach with your pupils once this has been achieved with staff:

- **Autonomy:** Children need to feel trusted. You can manage the level of autonomy you give them if you know them well.

- **Recognition:** Everyone likes to be recognised for getting things right, and this includes pupils. Recognition can be in the form of a smile, a thumbs up or a caring nod. It does not have to involve a tangible reward – stickers, house points, etc. If a pupil is emotionally invested in you, then the best reward they can get is your personal and genuine recognition.

---

5   This model has been created following conversation with and influenced by Dr Phil Wood of Bishop Grosseteste University. See also: Phil Wood, Rethinking Time in the Workload Debate, *Management in Education*, 33(2) (2019): 86–90; Phil Wood, Dave Whitaker – Unconditional Positive Regard: Developing High-Quality Alternative Provision, *Management in Education*, 33(3) (2019): 147–149.

Setting the tone with staff

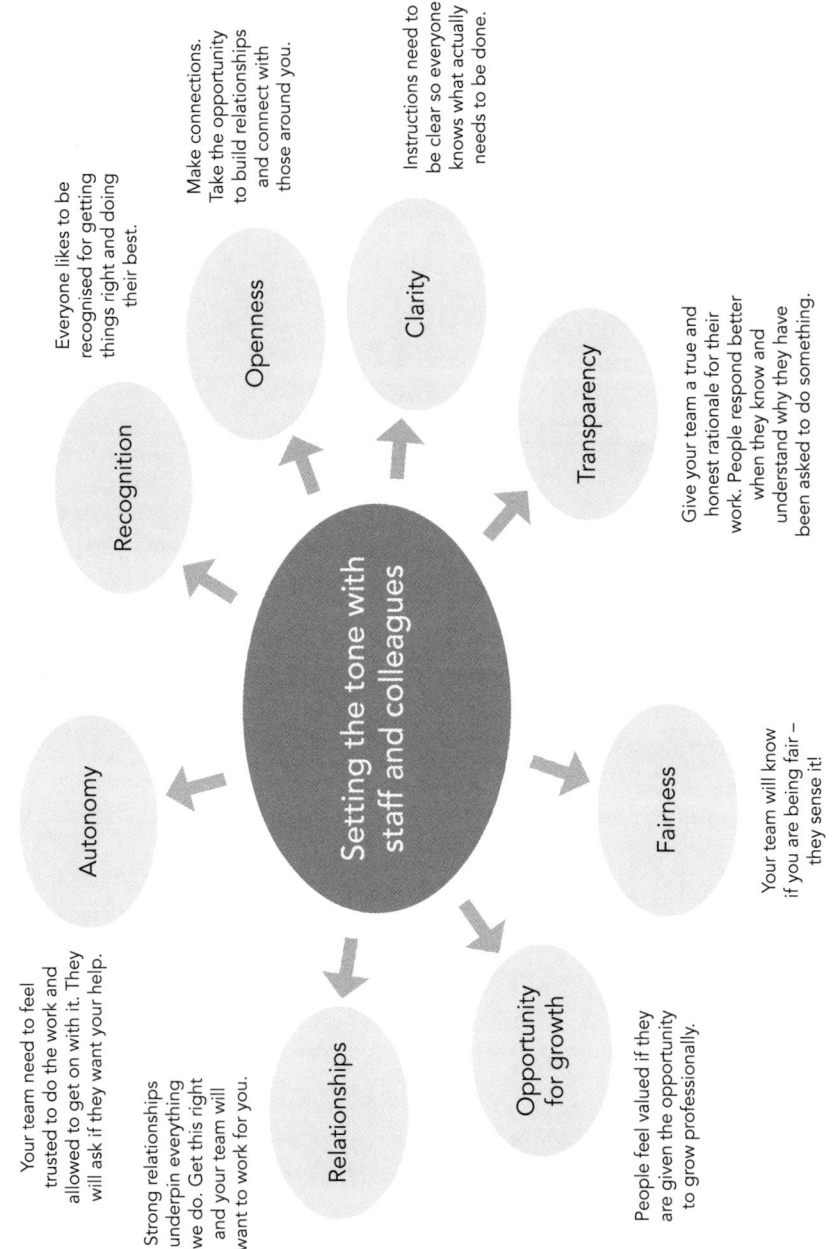

Setting the tone with staff and colleagues

Clarity
Instructions need to be clear so everyone knows what actually needs to be done.

Openness
Make connections. Take the opportunity to build relationships and connect with those around you.

Recognition
Everyone likes to be recognised for getting things right and doing their best.

Transparency
Give your team a true and honest rationale for their work. People respond better when they know and understand why they have been asked to do something.

Fairness
Your team will know if you are being fair – they sense it!

Autonomy
Your team need to feel trusted to do the work and allowed to get on with it. They will ask if they want your help.

Relationships
Strong relationships underpin everything we do. Get this right and your team will want to work for you.

Opportunity for growth
People feel valued if they are given the opportunity to grow professionally.

- **Openness:** Make connections with the pupils. This is an opportunity to give the children something of yourself on an emotional level. Being open and letting the children know about you as a person will help create a strong connection. It is possible to remain professional but allow the children to know what makes you tick. Being open with them makes you 'real' and easier to connect with.

- **Clarity:** Ensure that your instructions are clear and relatively simple. Personalise and make reasonable adjustments where needed. What you may think is a simple instruction or concept may be baffling to someone else, and you have to constantly be aware of your own clarity.

- **Transparency:** Let the pupils know why you are doing things the way you are. Allow them insight into your thinking, the curriculum and the sequence of your planning. If they understand it, they are far more likely to buy into it. Do not assume that they know what you are thinking. And do not be critical if they do not. The skill of the teacher is to be clear and open about our expectations. Remove the fog. Children will respond better if they know why they have been asked to do something.

- **Fairness:** This is a cornerstone of behaviour management. Children do not like to feel a sense of injustice. You need to consider this in every interaction and manage expectations accordingly. If you are open and transparent, the children will understand that you are being fair and reasonable.

- **Opportunity for growth:** We need to raise our expectations for the most challenging pupils. We must be careful that we do not dumb down expectations in order to create compliance. The skill of the teacher is to see and exploit every opportunity to help even the most challenging of pupils to grow. This will raise their confidence and in turn give them more self-esteem.

- **Relationships:** Strong relationships underpin all that we do. You have been open with the children, so now you can build the relationships. You can show warmth and have fun. You can challenge and support your pupils. Get this bit right and even the most challenging pupil will work for you.

Chapter Three

No excuses, plenty of fear

Fear is the path to the dark side. Fear leads to anger. Anger leads to hate. Hate leads to suffering.

Yoda[1]

No excuses and zero tolerance

We each make choices in our approach to managing behaviour. However, sometimes the choices are restricted to some degree because we work in a system in which our approach is underpinned by a non-negotiable policy. This is imposed on us by the system, whether we believe in it or not. The 'system' may be the school, an academy trust or, indeed, education policy itself. If we are working within a structure that we do not fully believe in, it makes the daily challenge of behaviour management stressful and tests our values constantly. We are therefore left with the difficult choice of whether to flout school policy or compromise our own beliefs and values. We become finely balanced on a 'values seesaw'.[2] Too often we see both teachers and leaders trapped by a system that they do not truly or fully believe in. This could be a system in which policy always outweighs values. Put simply, there is always a stringent response to a behaviour incident, irrespective of the context. This is also known as a 'no-excuses' behaviour policy. These policies occupy the same place on the spectrum as 'zero-tolerance' behaviour policies – they are essentially the same thing by a different name – and are promoted in many schools as being an appropriate and successful way of managing behaviour. You may have noticed that more recently schools have adopted 'warm-strict' policies – this is essentially zero tolerance in disguise. It could even be argued that the adoption of this term

1   *Star Wars: Episode I – The Phantom Menace*, dir. George Lucas (1999).
2   For more on this, see: Dave Whitaker, The Values Seesaw. In Ian Gilbert (ed.), *There is Another Way: The Second Big Book of Independent Thinking* (Carmarthen: Independent Thinking Press, 2015), pp. 49–54.

is a way of portraying a different image of a no-excuses policy – essentially a public relations exercise. Using the term 'warm' makes it seem more acceptable; the same dog, only washed!

The choices of individual teachers and leaders directly influence the practice of the behaviour policy and the tone of the overall behaviour approach. Too often we see adults using fear to control children; scaring them with the threat of punishment. This fuels anxiety in even the most well-behaved children. Children being scared in school is simply not acceptable. However, it seems that this methodology is increasingly being championed, and strict compliance is even seen as a positive thing.

Harsh punishment or meaningful deterrent?

In 1986 caning was outlawed in British state schools. Corporal punishment was previously a common sanction, with children being hit on the palm of their hand with a cane, for example. At the time this was an acceptable practice – it was, historically, viewed as an appropriate sanction following a behaviour incident. We must ask ourselves how effective this method was and whether it changed behaviour at all. Do children change their behaviour because they do not want to risk receiving a harsh punishment? If the cane was successful as a deterrent to misbehaviour, then there would have been no need to ban it, as it would have only existed as a threat and a preventative measure. As it happens, it was outlawed for being barbaric and, essentially, unsuccessful. So, even hitting children with a stick does not work. Indeed, if harsh punishments worked then surely there would be far less serious crime in the USA, as the threat of the death penalty would be a meaningful deterrent?

Although we now cannot hit children with sticks, it has been deemed appropriate to find replacement forms of punishment that can also be perceived as harsh – intentionally so, by some. These punishments are used as a deterrent and are intended to create fear. The use of isolation booths is widespread and seen by many as the panacea of behaviour management: strict discipline with increasing levels of sanctions that include sitting silently in a booth for up to six hours a day, sometimes for days on end.

A mechanism for removal from class for disruptive and/or dangerous behaviour is essential for the health and safety of other children and staff. Isolation from other pupils, when delivered as an intervention and for short periods of time, also has its place in a successful behaviour policy. However, we must ask ourselves whether it is ever appropriate for children to spend hour after hour, day after day, sitting in silence, facing the wall in a high-sided booth – sometimes for having done nothing more than break the school's hairstyle policy. We must also ask whether this, as an intervention, actually works. If it does work, does it work for all? We must empathise with these children. Try to imagine what it would be like to spend six hours sitting silently in a booth facing the wall. No talking or interaction, limited toilet breaks and no hot lunch. Imagine having to do this for days on end just because your hair is too short. Also, imagine how you would feel if that happened to your own child. How tolerant of the behaviour policy would you be?

I once had a very moving conversation with a head teacher as she was experiencing a particular struggle with the behaviour policy at her school. She was kind and compassionate and understood the challenges of the school and the community it served. She was doing her very best, every day, to make her school a kind and caring environment in which all children could thrive. However, her behaviour policy was non-negotiable. It was a policy established and set by an academy trust and imposed on every school in the trust without any exception or flexibility. It took no account of local context and was set up around a no-excuses, zero-tolerance, sanctions-driven system. Every infringement of the rules had a predetermined related sanction, with an escalation for repeat offences. Detentions, isolation booths, fixed-period exclusions and, ultimately, permanent exclusion were used to establish discipline and fast-track improvement. This specific problem played out due to the lack of flexibility in the system. Children were automatically placed in thirty-minute detentions for not having the correct equipment for class, for example, and a raft of other small-scale offences. Children arriving without a pen were immediately sanctioned and expected to complete a detention that evening after school. The children, who very often did not even own a pen, responded in two main ways.

First, some accepted the sanction and dutifully attended the detention. However, it was clear that this punishment was not really changing their behaviour, as the children would sit through numerous and repeated detentions for the same offences. They often came without equipment and just grew to accept their punishment as part of their school lives. School data showed many repeat offenders who continued to arrive at school without equipment, with uniform infringements or without their homework – they just carried on having detentions. Many of these children were from vulnerable families, were in receipt of free school meals and/or had additional needs.

Second, there were the children who just did not attend the detention – and there were many of these. They simply decided that they were not going to attend and left school at the end of the day regardless. These children immediately fell into the sanction escalation policy and were issued with a day in an isolation booth. The problem escalated quickly as the school did not have the 'booth capacity' to deal with demand. With only six booths and forty children requiring isolation, the booths were quickly overwhelmed, and the school needed a solution. They needed to 'flatten the curve', so to speak, and reduce the level of peak demand. They were accumulating isolations so quickly that they needed action, fast. They had choices: review the behaviour policy, increase the number of booths, or create a waiting list. They preferred the final option. Children were waiting for up to eight weeks to be placed in isolation. Option one was out of the question as it relied on a trust-wide review and changes, which was never going to happen. Option two was impossible simply because of a lack of available space. Option three meant children were serving punishments for 'crimes' they committed eight weeks ago – often just forgetting a pen.

Surely, if children are repeatedly getting detentions for not bringing a pen, we need to look at why they do not bring a pen. Do they have a pen to bring? Maybe we should consider helping them to get a pen or, dare I say it, give them one? Have you ever genuinely forgotten something? Would making you do a worksheet in silence for half an hour help you not to forget it again? If you lived in a house in which there were no pens, your parents could not read or write, and there was no money for food or to pay the bills, would spending half an hour after school doing maths help you to have a pen next week?

Some schools with caring and supportive cultures do use booths for isolation. However, most of these schools will use the booths only for very limited time outs for children to settle and calm after an incident – often for genuine behaviour regulation. They will also be used in conjunction with a restorative approach, and the pupils will be supported by a skilled member of staff with the intention of repair and reparation, rather than harsh punishment and deterrent. This is done in a responsible, time-limited and humane way. They also probably give pens to children who do not have their own.

We can consider adult human behaviour and how we respond to rules and their associated punishments. If a driver is going too fast and sees a speed camera, they automatically slow the car down. They do not want a fine, and this punishment is non-negotiable – no excuses. After they have passed the camera, they speed up again. However, if they are caught speeding and are both fined *and* instructed to attend a speed-awareness course, they are more likely to change their behaviour than if they are just issued with a fine.

Regulation and reward

If you find a lost purse on the road that contains cash, what do you do? Do you take the cash out, put it in your pocket and throw the purse away or do you try to find the owner and return the purse? On returning the purse do you expect a reward or are you returning the purse because it is simply the right thing to do? Culturally, we hope everyone would return the purse with the contents intact, and not expect a reward.

Therefore, we need to make sure that we do not have an over-reliance on rewards. Rewards definitely have their place, but what do we mean by 'reward'? Do we want children to behave either because they fear a sanction or because they desire a material reward? Or do we want children to behave because they know and understand that behaving is the right thing to do in their society or community? Do you, as a responsible member of society, only abide by the law because of fear of sanction or because you desire some sort of reward for compliance? Believe it or not, rewards can be a problem, and this is something that we will cover later. Punishments and sanctions are, by their very nature, an intervention. If we are to employ interventions, then we must be convinced that they work, or else what is the point?

Try this

- If you are a school leader, examine your school's behaviour data and analyse the number of repeat offenders. How many children change their behaviour following a sanction and how many go on to offend repeatedly? Use detention, isolation and fixed-term-exclusion data to really see if sanctions really are working.

- If you are a teacher, then analyse your class data and look at how effective your sanctions are – do they work? Are the same children repeat offenders?

Punitive consistency

The success of zero-tolerance and no-excuses behaviour policies is predicated on creating fear and worry. They rely on a significant proportion of the pupil population being constantly anxious. Zero tolerance relies on children being scared. Even the most compliant, hard-working and personable pupil may be harbouring a level of anxiety that is a direct response to a sanctions-driven, no-excuses policy.

Let's look at another example. A group of children arrived five minutes late to school. The no-excuses behaviour policy states that if a child is late, they receive a thirty-minute detention – no excuses. The children were late because the bus was late. It is the only bus they can get. They all live in a middle-class, rural village outside town. It's a part of the catchment area where prior attainment levels are generally high and the secondary school actively encourages children from this village to attend, as their academic contribution will have a positive impact on progress measures. The school knew that the bus was late and that six children, all from that same village, were therefore late. But the teacher said, 'Sorry, guys, I know it's unfair, but I have to give you all a detention because I've given everyone else who was late a detention too.' They all received the thirty-minute detention. Right or wrong? This is a great example of how a teacher might not believe in the system thar they are obliged to administer; they might be aware of how unjust it really is, but they still have to go through the motions. The result of this imposition was that six children, none of whom felt they had done anything wrong, all ended up, right then, feeling resentful towards school. Most of these children had never received a detention before and were hard-working and diligent pupils. However, rules are rules – consistency wins (but should it?).

Discretion is therefore a word that is essentially absent from a zero-tolerance approach. Punishment, with no excuses, is seen as a strength and discretion seen as a weakness. Extenuating circumstances (such as the bus being late) do nothing to prevent the imposition of a predetermined sanction. Zero tolerance hijacks the term 'consistency' and uses it as a justification for being unreasonably harsh. Consistency is an important aspect of behaviour management, but not necessarily in this case.

Abi, aged 15, lived with her mum and two younger siblings, who were still at primary school – two different ones. Abi's mum was a heroin addict; she was loving and caring but struggled, daily, with addiction and associated mental health problems. She therefore relied heavily on Abi, who was an unofficial carer for her mum and brothers. She cooked, she washed clothes, she did the shopping, and she took the boys to school every day. Abi's own school had a no-excuses policy for late arrival. The school were aware of Abi's circumstances. They knew that she took her siblings to school every day and that her mum was struggling to parent effectively. Abi would wake early every morning, feed and dress her brothers and begin the morning routine of delivering them to two separate schools before making her own way. She was often late because it was practically impossible to organise the logistics of the morning routine. The only way she could possibly arrive on time was to run, after dropping off her youngest brother. She would receive detentions, with no excuses, almost daily. This would often escalate into arguments with teachers as she perceived this as an injustice and something that she could not control. Her first daily interaction with school and the adults there was always negative and punitive. This would then result in time in an isolation booth and, inevitably, a fixed-term exclusion. Abi was on the verge of permanent exclusion essentially because she was caring for and looking after her mum and brothers. Abi's grandma, in floods of tears, came to see me to ask if there was anything I could do to help. It was heartbreaking and all I wanted to do was get Abi to come to my school – that's really what her grandma wanted too. Unfortunately, that did not happen.

An Education Endowment Foundation (EEF) report, *Improving Behaviour in Schools*, clearly states that there is no evidence to support the success of zero-tolerance behaviour policies.[3] However, they remain widely used in English schools and held in high regard by the Department for Education – the very organisation that funds the EEF's research.

Try this

Ask yourself the following questions. Reflect and satisfy yourself that your own values are driving your decisions and choices.

- Is it OK to have a policy that makes some children in your school scared?

- Is it OK to be part of a policy in which the fear of a sanction is the fundamental driver to the success of a behaviour management system?

- Do you really believe in a no-excuses approach, or do you just tolerate it?

- Do you really believe in the use of isolation booths or do you support it because it makes your working life simple, binary and easier to manage?

- Do you think zero-tolerance approaches will actually change long-term behaviour?

- Do you think it's OK that zero-tolerance, no-excuses styles of behaviour management do not consider the child's background and domestic circumstances?

- What are we trying to achieve by using a no-excuses approach?

- Do you feel that asking yourself these questions is important?

---

3   Igraine Rhodes and Michelle Long, *Improving Behaviour in Schools: Guidance Report* (London: Education Endowment Foundation, 2019). Available at: https://educationendowmentfoundation.org.uk/tools/guidance-reports/improving-behaviour-in-schools/.

If your answer to the final question is 'no', then it is probably best if you stop reading now and send this book back – you could try and get a refund (or maybe carry on reading and see if you change your mind).

In the 2002 film *Goodbye, Mr Chips*, based on the novella by James Hilton[4] about the life of a schoolteacher in the 1930s, there is a discussion about how punishment does not work and how other solutions must be found. Chips' wife, Mrs Chipping, highlights the need to use persuasion over force. To emphasise this, she quotes from one of Aesop's Fables 'The North Wind and the Sun'.

> Headmaster, do you know the fable of The Sun and the North Wind?
>
> The Sun and the North Wind were arguing one day as to who possessed the greatest powers. 'Observe,' said the North Wind. 'Observe that man down there, see how I will blow his coat from his shoulders.' So, the North Wind blew, icier and icier but of course the man simply wrapped his coat even tighter round his shoulders. And then the Sun gently said, 'North Wind, you've had your opportunity, please allow me.' And the sun shone, warmer and warmer and the man took off his coat.[5]

If we do not rely on fear, then we must find another way. Instead of zero tolerance, let us try tolerance and compassion. Instead of no excuses, let us try to understand the context and show empathy. But, let us be clear, when exploring this 'other way', we never compromise on our expectations, rigour and standards.

> Anger, fear, aggression. The dark side are they. Once you start down the dark path, forever will it dominate your destiny.
>
> Yoda[6]

---

4 James Hilton, *Goodbye, Mr Chips* (London: Hodder & Stoughton, 1934).
5 *Goodbye, Mr Chips*, dir. Stuart Orme (2002).
6 *Star Wars: Episode V – The Empire Strikes Back*, dir. George Lucas (1980).

Chapter Four

Rewards, sanctions and praise

When we behave well, it's rarely because we want a reward or because we fear a punishment, it's because behaving with consideration towards other people comes naturally to us.

Philippa Perry[1]

Beyond the behaviourist approach

Traditionally, many schools have taken a clear behaviourist approach to managing behaviour and 'enforcing' discipline. This is often reflected in teacher training and in the work of numerous consultants and 'experts' who deliver training in schools and write books and blogs that are read by thousands of aspirant and experienced teachers and leaders.

Strict discipline is associated with compliance at all costs. Sanctions are therefore put in place to help enforce compliance, and rewards simply allow the celebration of conformity. The word 'discipline' implies subservience, and, to many, this is traditionally what we must aspire to achieve in schools. However, subservience, by definition, implies being less important than something or someone else – a willingness to obey unquestioningly. Is this genuinely what we wish to achieve in schools, or would we prefer children to engage and conform because they know and understand that it is the right thing to do in that community? Surely, we would get more satisfaction from knowing that children are 'doing the right thing' without them fearing punishment if they do not. Also, would it not be better if children complied because they knew it was the right thing to do, rather than because they desire a material reward?

---

1   Philippa Perry, *The Book You Wish Your Parents Had Read (and Your Children Will Be Glad That You Did)* (London: Penguin Life, 2019), pp. 177.

Put simply, the behaviourist approach sees behaviour from an observational perspective: a 'judgement' is made on whether that behaviour is appropriate and therefore acceptable. In essence, we assume that the behaviour is a choice that's being made and that rational decisions are influencing the individual's responses. Behaviourist approaches rely very much on an external view of a person's actions and ignore the emotion, feelings and thinking that may result in them displaying challenging behaviour. This approach very much emphasises right from wrong, seeing everything as a black-or-white situation. It is clear, straightforward and easy to measure. It allows us to make easy judgements and employ uncomplicated responses, and it fits nicely into systems and policies. It can be underpinned by a clear system of sanctions and rewards. Data is easy to collect and analyse, reports are easy to compile and 'evidence' of inappropriate behaviour is clear. If you need to gather evidence to inform exclusions, or to satisfy an Ofsted inspection, then this approach is perfect – if that is your goal.

The behaviourist approach is easy and simple. As a teacher, having a clear, prescribed set of rules, with associated sanctions and rewards, is what many schools aspire to. It is also easy for leaders. Behaviour policy and its associated systems are easy if a purely behaviourist approach is taken. Leaders can give clear instructions, there is no confusion for staff and it is therefore easy to administer. So why should we look any further? It would be unfair to say that it does not work – it just does not work for everyone. So, if we take the easy approach, there will be unintentional consequences and some children will fail, be excluded and disappear into the behaviour black hole. In many schools this is considered acceptable; it is not an unintentional consequence but an accepted way of working. The school knows that some children will fail, and they accept that and embrace exclusion as a tolerable, even intentional, end point – even if they do not admit it publicly.

The problem is that children are complex; therefore, managing their behaviour with simplistic approaches will not work in every case and the system will inevitably fail for the most complicated, and often most vulnerable, children – and there are a surprisingly high number of these in every school.

If we want to remove sanctions as our default position as teachers, then we need to be skilled, compassionate, understanding, empathetic, caring, kind, assertive, genuine, authentic, accepting and determined. We need to be ambitious for our pupils, set high standards and support those children who find communication a challenge. We need to build strong, authentic and lasting relationships – then we do not need to rely on sanctions. So, we have a dilemma: we want success for all our pupils, but do we take the easy road or the hard road? Or is there an argument for a bit of both?

Intrinsic and extrinsic motivation

Children must be motivated to behave, just as adults must too. We can either be intrinsically motivated, and therefore possess an innate (or learnt?) desire to do the right thing, or we need extrinsic motivation, meaning we fear a sanction or crave a material reward. When looking at these options in their most simplistic form, surely we must agree that we should predominately desire intrinsic motivation?

The EEF states that:

> Extrinsic motivation – in the form of external influences such as gaining rewards and praise – is useful to address some minor misbehaviours or to encourage positive behaviour. Teachers can use tangible techniques such as rewards and sanctions, or less tangible strategies such as praise and criticism, to improve motivation, behaviour, and learning. However, it is intrinsic motivation, or self-motivation, that is crucial to improving resilience, achieving goals, and ultimately is the key determiner to success. Children who are intrinsically motivated achieve better and are less likely to misbehave.[2]

With this in mind, where is the evidence to suggest that children are more likely to comply with rules when there are high-stakes sanctions in place?

What is noticeable about the research conducted by the EEF is their claim that extrinsic motivation is useful when dealing with minor misbehaviours. In schools, the serious challenge is with behaviours that we would consider more severe, and therefore rewards and sanctions have little or no impact on behaviour change. The use of a sanctions system will prevent some minor infringements (it may also cause

---

2   Rhodes and Long, Improving Behaviour in Schools, p. 18.

unnecessary anxiety in some children) or give us a short-term quick fix. Similarly, the use of a reward system will motivate some children to follow the rules. However, if these systems worked as we wish them to, then schools would never need to use permanent exclusion – the combination of sanctions and motivational rewards would prevent anyone needing to be excluded. So, does it really work?

Relationships as a motivational factor

Self-control, and therefore self-motivation, needs to be encouraged and supported in school – and this starts with authentic relationships. Clinical psychologist Kim Golding uses the term 'connection before correction' when supporting parents who are dealing with children suffering from early developmental trauma.[3] Make sure that your behaviour, in the classroom or the school corridor, demonstrates this principle. Children look to adults for an emotional connection. Adults, if they are not careful, will look to form more academic or formal connections, sometimes neglecting the emotional bond, but then still expect children to engage with them. Children, on the other hand, will struggle to engage without that emotional connection with their teacher. Either way, there may be a deficit that can result in non-compliance and therefore challenging behaviour. Adults need to work hard to develop connections, and once the connection is there, they can correct behaviour successfully without the need for reward or sanction – in fact, the reward, to the child, is the connection.

Most children in PRUs or alternative provision (AP) are there because they have been excluded from mainstream education. They are placed in specialist provision because the system has not worked for them. They have not responded to sanction- or consequence-based systems, their behaviour has not improved, and they have found themselves needing specialist intervention. Most of these pupils are 'rule-breakers' – they smoke, they do not wear appropriate uniform, they do not complete homework, they arrive late, they truant, they swear openly and habitually. How is it possible to change the behaviour of such children when they arrive in a PRU

---

3   Kim S. Golding, Connection Before Correction: Supporting Parents to Meet the Challenges of Parenting Children who have been Traumatised within their Early Parenting Environments, *Children Australia*, 40(2) (2015): 152–159.

with already entrenched behaviours and join their peers who are there for the same reasons?

I often reflect on and admire a particular Key Stage 4 teacher who came to work in my school having left mainstream after becoming disillusioned with the clinical and systematic zero-tolerance behaviour policy he was obliged to follow. He had ten pupils in his class – all of them excluded from mainstream and lacking motivation, self-belief and self-control. They had come through a school system that constantly punished them, and they were immune to sanctions. We had nothing in our armoury except relational practice and this teacher embraced it. He knew that the only way he could change the behaviour of his class was if he helped them to want to change. He built such strong relationships with that group that he created an emotional, authentic connection with them all – as a group and as individuals.

He changed the behaviour of that class because they wanted to behave for him. He asked them to stop smoking – they stopped. He asked them to stop swearing – they stopped. He motivated them to complete their classwork, not because they feared a sanction, but because they knew it was what their teacher wanted, and it was the right thing to do. He transformed a group of extremely challenging and disillusioned teenagers into a successful class, who supported each other and were intrinsically motivated. He was meticulous at conveying his high expectations and implemented clear routines and structures. He never 'allowed' poor behaviour, and he challenged everything he felt was inappropriate. Those children developed self-belief and self-control because of a genuine and authentic human connection with an adult who they respected and believed in. Not once was this a 'soft' approach; not once was challenging behaviour tolerated or accepted. This is happening in great PRUs, APs and SEMH special schools every day – it can work in mainstream too and is successful in many.

One of the most common questions I have been asked by teachers and leaders in PRUs or SEMH schools is 'How can I stop them smoking?' Often, the default approach is to want to use a sanction, and they ask me what is appropriate. The answer is always the same: we can only stop them smoking if they want to. Sanctions are meaningless; they only damage relationships and breed resentment. These children do not care about or respond to sanctions. The only way they will genuinely want to stop smoking is if they believe in you and believe that you want them to stop. In most cases they will not stop smoking entirely, they will just make sure that they do not smoke at school. Your emotional connection is the most powerful change agent. If the children respect you, they will respond by changing their behaviour – even the most challenging children. Their 'reward' is to see you pleased with them – to earn mutual respect.

Reward systems and their negative, unintended consequences

Many schools use long-term rewards to attempt to motivate pupils and improve behaviour and attendance. I must make it clear that I am not opposed to the use of rewards per se, but feel that we need to consider whether they genuinely work and whether they can even be a problem. For example, many secondary schools (and now even some primary schools) organise a prom for their leavers. I hear many stories of children who have been excluded from the prom because they have failed to meet the 'required standard' of behaviour or attendance. In many cases, these children have written off going to the prom from an early stage. They do not believe that they will reach the required standard, and therefore the reward is demotivating and unachievable – the goal is distant and unattainable, so why bother? Some of those children will, in order to protect their own self-esteem, actively try to fall well below the required standard. Let's face it, for these children it is better not to even try than to try your hardest and miss out by falling short. Some children from disadvantaged backgrounds will also avoid the prom – and so misbehaving is a way of being excluded and saving face – as they cannot afford a flash suit or a ballgown and a plush limousine to transport them there. By its very nature, the prom can be unintentionally exclusive, cause anxiety and be a very negative way to give closure to a school career. For the vast majority, the school prom is an excellent finish to your time at school; to the silent minority, the prom is an event to try to block out and forget.

Non-uniform days can also be a real problem for children who do not own a pair of fashionable trainers or the latest branded hoody. Many vulnerable children will truant non-uniform days or will arrive in their uniform claiming that they forgot. There is evidence showing that Christmas Jumper Day can have an adverse effect on the attendance of the most vulnerable children, even though, of course, the innocent intention of the school is to have fun.[4] It is far easier for a child to take ridicule from their peers for 'forgetting' than for not having the 'right' clothes. And many parents cannot afford to buy a Christmas jumper – or in many cases they cannot be bothered to. I vividly remember seeing this happen when I oversaw an inclusion unit in a mainstream secondary school. Three times a year there was a non-uniform day and on all three of those days the attendance of my pupils fell dramatically.

Many primary schools still use traffic-light behaviour systems on the walls of their classrooms. In secondary schools, teachers will write children's names on the board or wall to signify warnings for unacceptable behaviour. When a child misbehaves or fails to follow instructions, their name is moved next to the red light or, in some cases, the dark thunder cloud. Those children who are doing well, completing their work and following instructions have their names next to the green light or the sunshine. The names are there, for all to see, on the classroom wall.

Imagine if that system was used by the head teacher for staff appraisal in your school. In the staffroom there is a traffic-light system on the wall. All those staff who are 'doing well' have their names next to the green traffic light for all to see. However, those who are struggling, on support plans or just going through a difficult time have their names next to the red light. Every day the head teacher comes into the staffroom and moves the names depending on how 'successful' you all are. In fact, they may have a whiteboard in the staffroom on which they write the names of those staff members who have been late or failed to hit a deadline for data or report submission. How would that make you feel? I am sure you would feel humiliated, angry and totally demotivated. I imagine that you would seriously consider a formal complaint or at the very least look for another job in a more compassionate environment. The simple question we must ask is: if that makes me feel like that, then how does it make the children feel?

---

4   See Martin George, Exclusive: Data reveals poor pupils' Xmas jumper shame, *TES* (31 May 2019). Available at: https://www.tes.com/news/exclusive-data-reveals-poor-pupils-xmas-jumper-shame; and https://opendataproject.org.uk/wp-content/uploads/2020/09/Christmas-Jumper-Day.pdf.

The power of praise

Using praise rather than reward allows us to move away from a material prize to a more relational and emotional enhancement. Praise expresses warm approval and admiration, whereas reward is a 'thing' given for recognition or achievement. Praise therefore means authentic and genuine relational recognition, and is a powerful motivator for children. Yes, rewards have their place, and this is by no means an anti-reward stance. This is simply an opportunity to encourage intrinsic responses and motivation in children that will help them change their behaviour and build resilience. Praise, coming from a respected adult, will generate a dopamine release in a child and we have already discussed how significant this is. Remember, the praise needs to be genuine and the children need to believe that you care. Praise can also be powerful when subtle, and simple non-verbal gestures or a quiet whisper of congratulation in a child's ear can be real motivators. A phone call home to parents or carers that strengthens the personal connection and relationship with the child can also really help. Using praise authentically is so important here, and Alfie Kohn warns us that overpraising can lead to children changing their behaviour for a short while but showing no long-term commitment to that change.[5] He also cautions us that some children may react negatively to positive reinforcement by becoming openly defiant or withdrawing in a show of passive resistance. Hence the importance of knowing the children well and personalising your strategy as sophisticatedly as possible. Furthermore, he stresses the importance of aiming for intrinsic motivation when it comes to both learning and behaviour.

---

5   Alfie Kohn, *Punished by Rewards: The Trouble with Gold Stars, Incentive Plans, A's, Praise, and Other Bribes* (Boston, MA: Houghton Mifflin Company, 1993).

Humiliation and shame

We need to be aware of how humiliation can be inadvertently used to drive a reward or sanction process. Unachievable rewards, as well as the use of charts and public exposure that attempts to change behaviour, have long-lasting negative impacts on children, particularly those who have a history of trauma or anxiety. Unfortunately, in some cases, humiliation is actively used as a technique to control behaviour and is seen as perfectly acceptable.

Charts are great if they are purely positive, and I have seen excellent examples in classrooms of teachers using them to celebrate and praise great work and behaviour. However, too many times I have seen children being publicly shamed and humiliated – often unintentionally, with the teacher believing it to be appropriate, effective and even motivational. The key here is to keep them positive – praising and rewarding the good stuff – even if you take small steps.

I have very mixed feelings about a technique that I once saw used by a teacher with her class of Year 9 scientists. With the intention of making her own work more efficient she produced a single feedback sheet for the whole class. On this sheet she highlighted the children who had achieved highly in their work. She also included a section in which she listed those who had not completed their homework or had poor grades. She created a box for reviewing the presentation skills of the class, and even gave Jono his own personal section to note that he had stuck his work in his book upside down. Poor Jono was inadvertently shamed that day, as all thirty children were issued with the sheet to take home. This teacher was not intentionally trying to shame the class (hence my mixed feelings), but she had clearly got it wrong. The children themselves even named this the 'Sheet of Shame'. Upon reflection, the teacher realised her mistake and the Sheet of Shame was never seen again.

I was once visiting a mainstream secondary school and was taken for a tour of the classrooms by the principal. The school was calm and well-ordered; classrooms and corridors where quiet; and children were generally compliant (however, the atmosphere did feel a bit stale and subdued). On arrival in one particular Year 8 classroom, the teacher was in the middle of an instruction or explanation and as we entered the room fell silent. The children were visibly scared of the principal. This took me by surprise, even though I had visited many schools and been in hundreds of classrooms. He was an imposing figure, at over six-feet tall and wearing a sharp blue suit and shiny brown brogues. As the class sat still – upright and straight faced – the principal slowly raised his arm and pointed to the whiteboard at the front of the classroom. There, in a specially allocated 'consequences' corner, was written the names of two boys. As he pointed, he sternly said, 'You two boys, stand up, now.'

I was immediately uncomfortable with the tone and the nature of the request. As the rest of the class sat rigid, with even the teacher frozen at the front of the class, the boys stood, hands by their sides, their heads bowed. The next instruction, after a slight pause – clearly designed to add tension – was simply: 'Outside, now.' The boys, without hesitation but resisting eye contact, walked out of the classroom followed by the principal and then me, trailing reluctantly and uncomfortably. I did not really know where to put myself or how to respond. The boys stood against the corridor wall, hands by their sides, their heads bowed. The principal stood near them, bent over slightly to be level with their faces and began what can only be described as a bollocking. I do not use this term lightly, but there is no other way to describe it.

He was shouting loudly in their faces, warning them of the serious consequences that they would face if they failed to behave. He made it clear that the school would not tolerate any form of defiance and that they could expect to be excluded if it continued. He had no idea what they had actually done and was responding purely to the fact that their names were on the board. By this time, I had walked away from the scene. I could not bring myself to be associated with this tactic and felt uncomfortable and awkward. This was not an isolated incident; it was clearly a system that was in place and part of a measured, regular response in that school. The boys were physically shaking as they were sent back into class. Humiliation had been used as a behaviour management approach – condoned, even enforced, by the principal – and was clearly an unwritten but championed element of that 'successful' school's behaviour policy. All I ask is that we question this and consider the viability and morality. Success, yes, but at any cost?

Restoration, not revenge

As adults working in schools, we must resist seeking revenge or holding a grudge against a child. We must ask ourselves why we are considering a punishment before administering a sanction. Our own honest self-reflection may expose an initial desire for revenge, and this needs to be stopped. A sanction (although I hate that word), if appropriate, needs to be logical and restorative. In other words, it needs to help change a behaviour, restore a relationship or fix a problem, and it needs to link logically to the initial incident. It is imperative that we are honest with ourselves and able to stop our own personal feelings from driving our decision making when dealing with inappropriate behaviour.

In fact, we could adopt the term 'logical response', rather than sanction. This way, an adult can work with a child in a logical and relational way that allows a consequence to be delivered that not only seems fair but is delivered with a restorative emphasis so that relationships remain intact. This, once again, allows us to use the social discipline window, which we explored in Chapter Two.

Liam was in Year 7 and an extremely volatile and difficult young man. He had been excluded from three primary schools and his home life was complex. He had been exposed to traumatic events and environmental challenges ever since birth, including criminal activity and drug abuse. He was physically injured before even being born due to his mother's exposure to domestic violence during pregnancy. He would quickly fall into crisis over very small and seemingly insignificant things. His window of tolerance was narrow, and he struggled to sustain long periods of concentration. On one occasion, whilst in crisis mode, he angrily left his classroom after tipping over tables, throwing chairs and punching walls. Once outside he began kicking windows, lots of them. The windows were strong so the only real damage he did was to smear them with mud from his dirty shoes. Eventually he tired himself out and stopped, lying on the grass exhausted. I was asked to help with Liam as I knew him well and we had a trusting relationship that had been forged over many months of incident management, tears, hugs and lots of talking.

Liam sat in my office, calm but sullen. He knew that he had acted in an extreme way and that he could not just return to class as if nothing had happened. He knew that we needed to reflect, and he was fully aware that we did not just allow this sort of behaviour to go without consequence. I knew that I had to go through a simple restorative process with him and hopefully reach a position where logical intervention could be used. My aim was to use the social discipline window as my framework for a conversation that would allow Liam to reflect on his behaviour, empathise with others in the situation and put things right – that was my why.

I started by simply asking Liam to tell me what had happened. Of course, I knew exactly what had happened because the staff had already told me. However, I needed Liam to tell me his view of events as this created an opportunity for him to reflect. He was able to tell me in detail how the incident occurred and what he had done. It was a very honest account that allowed me to prompt him further with my next question. I asked him to tell me who else had been affected and how they might be feeling. Liam now began to empathise with others. He told me that his teachers and teaching assistants had been upset by his actions. He explained how the other children had been disturbed and the class had been disrupted. He even told me how he must have upset George, the caretaker, because all the windows were now covered in mud from his shoes. Everyone loved George: he had been at the school forever and had a brilliant relationship with all the children. When Liam reflected on the state of the dirty windows, this particularly bothered him. After briefly discussing the people who were affected, I simply asked Liam, 'What can we do to put things right?' I purposely used the word 'we', rather than 'you', because I wanted Liam to know that I was willing and able to help him put things right. We were operating in the 'with' box in the social discipline window and I wanted to make sure that we stayed there.

Liam wanted to put things right. He knew that he needed to apologise to the staff and was willing to do that genuinely. We made a plan for him to talk to his teacher – he wanted to do that; I was not directing him to. He was also worried about George and was feeling a sense of guilt about the muddy windows. He did not want George to resent him and told me that he felt bad about George having to clean the windows. This allowed me to ask a follow-up question that would again stimulate Liam's empathy.

I asked him who he thought should clean the windows. I was very careful not to direct him to volunteer himself as I wanted him to reach that conclusion on his own, which he did. I then asked him when he thought would be the best time to do it and, because he is not stupid, Liam indicated that he should probably do it during his maths lesson. After explaining that this was not appropriate, Liam suggested that it was probably best if he stayed behind after school and cleaned the windows so that George did not have to. I told him that that was a great idea and that I would organise a sponge and water. Liam spent forty-five minutes cleaning the windows. He did so with good grace and humility, and left school feeling supported, showing no resentment and looking forward to coming back in the morning. All relationships were intact, and he had shown genuine empathy. He had even done a detention, although I would prefer to call it a logical response. That said, after he left, George had to clean all the windows because Liam, with the best of intentions, had done such a bad job.

Try this

- If you are a leader with responsibility for the school's reward system, take some time to review how rewards may impact on the most vulnerable. Try to consider how the use of short-term, flexible rewards may have more of an impact on changing behaviour than rigid, structured systems. If you use house points or another merit system in your school, look at the data to see if children are actually being motivated by the rewards. Are the rewards differentiated so that they are genuinely inclusive?

- As an adult in the school, when referring to a behaviour intervention, consider this simple, powerful term that can be used to judge whether the intervention is appropriate: 'reasonable, proportionate and necessary'.[6] This is an excellent starting point for adults to think about when they reflect prior to the use of any punishment and for leaders to use when designing and implementing sanctions policies.

- If you are a teacher, start a 'praise wall' in your classroom. Highlight great stuff happening in the classroom and with the children, praising appropriately. Do not draw attention to the 'bad stuff' with traffic lights, or similar, but focus entirely on the positive praise. Praise the children who are doing well, rather than punishing and shaming those who are not.

---

6   This term is derived from Section 76 of the Criminal Justice and Immigration Act 2008. See https://www.legislation.gov.uk/ukpga/2008/4/section/76.

- Use one of the walls in your room to publicly praise the children. This could mean simply pinning their work to the wall, using stickers or even writing positive comments about them and their work. This will be motivational and celebratory without you having to rely on material rewards or prizes.

- If you are a leader responsible for behaviour training, adopt the term 'praise' rather than 'reward'. Take time to discuss the difference between praise and reward and how genuine, authentic praise can be more powerful than material reward when it comes from a trusted adult with a strong connection with a child.

- If you are a leader with responsibility for behaviour in your school, consider the use of logical responses rather than sanctions. Connect this to your school values and to a restorative approach (covered in Chapter Eight) and the social discipline window.

- If you are a head teacher or principal, set yourself the strategic goal of moving away from reward- and sanction-based behaviour practice and towards a relational approach.

Chapter Five

Behaviour policy – why bother?

Rules are not necessarily sacred; principles are.

Franklin D. Roosevelt[1]

What's in a behaviour policy?

A behaviour policy can either shackle or empower us. It can help us grow our skills and knowledge or it can tie us to a rigid set of instructions that prevent us from being our true selves. The school behaviour policy is the one key document that can make us happy, frustrated, confused or even angry. It can be used to hold us to account or be applied as an excuse or justification for an action or decision that we do not actually believe in. For teachers, it is a document beyond our control, imposed on us without consultation, consideration or appreciation. For some, it is taken literally and to the extreme; for others, it is ignored or morphed to suit their needs. In many cases it can be the reason to leave a school and look for work elsewhere, or the reason to join a school because it could be the solution to your career frustrations and problems. In many schools the behaviour policy will take account of the local perspective, but in others it will be a broad, trust-wide document that ignores context and has no localised nuance. In all cases, it is the most discussed policy in any staffroom and the one that fuels the most arguments. Everyone has a strong opinion about behaviour policy.

Whatever way we look at it, behaviour policies are controversial. They cover a spectrum of contention: respected colleagues and experienced professionals regularly disagree about style, content and approach. There are many school leaders who I

---

1   President Roosevelt addressing the Young Democratic Clubs of America in August 1935. Full transcript available at: https://www.presidency.ucsb.edu/documents/radio-address-the-young-democratic-clubs-america-0.

admire immensely but I fail to understand their approach to behaviour. The same policy can be viewed by some as successful and innovative and by others as a failure.

Fast-track school improvement is often linked directly to the implementation of zero-tolerance, no-excuses behaviour policies and, therefore, these approaches are held in high regard – without consideration of the consequences. Relational policies are slow burners, changing culture over time, and are often designed to meet the specific needs of a local community. However, as I have mentioned, they are viewed by some as ineffective and soft on discipline.

In order for everyone in the school to respect a behaviour policy and truly believe in its implementation, it must work. A successful behaviour policy must work for all, not just for some. It must be able to meet the needs of the school community and be the foundation of the school's culture. A school should be able to serve the community it finds itself in, rather than change its pupils to meet the needs of the school or trust. This does not mean that we accept lower standards or a lack of aspiration, but it does mean that we recognise that schools need to be adaptable, creative and committed to the children and families they serve. The behaviour policy can either prevent or allow this. A school should be proud of its behaviour policy and happy and confident to celebrate it, even if it is scrutinised publicly in the media. After all, behaviour policies are on school websites, and therefore in the public domain, so are open to examination and criticism. They are also viewed by parents and prospective employees as they make decisions about their choice of school or employer, respectively.

With this in mind, we can begin to look at what makes a great behaviour policy and consider the basis for a school's cultural construction around a solid platform of relational practice. This starts with the 'ownership' of the policy and once again asks us to consider the social discipline window. Behaviour policies should be co-constructed and regularly reviewed so that staff have ownership of what they do and can truly believe in it. Leaders can use this collaborative approach to develop the cultural buy-in they need for school-wide success. Behaviour policies that are done to, or done for, staff will never command the same commitment as those that are designed by all stakeholders, which includes the children themselves. As we have previously discussed, openness and transparency will empower both staff and pupils to own and respect the rules, standards, routines and expectations.

A great behaviour policy should be based on the following:

- High-quality classroom practice that allows *all* children to prosper and flourish.

- Expertise in restorative and relational practice, reflection and personalisation.

- Sophisticated approaches to exploring the reasons why children display challenging behaviour, developing strategies to address this, considering emotions and feelings, and being aware of trauma and anxiety.

- Delivery of high-quality special educational needs and disabilities (SEND) interventions and the development of appropriate strategies to support children with additional needs.

This is the starting point for your reflections on behaviour policy. Does your school's policy deliver on all these points? Including high-quality classroom practice in this list acknowledges the important role that teachers play in managing behaviour through their skills and ability to engage pupils. Investment in staff development and training will allow confident staff to be experts in the use of language and reflective practice. A great special educational needs and disabilities coordinator (SENDCO) will add massive value to the behaviour policy by incorporating and delivering strategies and interventions for children with SEMH difficulties. SENDCOs are too often seen as being responsible for education for children with additional needs but not actively involved in behaviour – they need to do both.

If the system you work in does not allow you to change the rules (and I am not advocating that you break the rules) then you must do your best to change the system. Then the rules will meet the needs of your school and your community. Many behaviour policies are founded on a sanctions-driven approach: a list of 'crimes' matching a menu of punishments. Some even have escalating punishments for repeat offenses with exclusion as the ultimate sanction. We know the serious consequences associated with exclusion (and for more on this see Chapter Nine), but many schools still use it as the basis for their policies – all roads lead to exclusion.

Reviewing and scrutinising your behaviour policy will allow you to reflect on its fitness for purpose and consider how inclusive it really is. It might also be time to consider what you are trying to achieve through your behaviour policy and the message it portrays to your school community. Do not forget that behaviour policies are in the public domain. They are available for scrutiny by the community via the school website. With this in mind, the behaviour policy sets the public tone for the school's culture and values and should be an opportunity to celebrate. Prospective employees will view the policy, as will Ofsted inspectors and visitors. If you are a leader, now could be the perfect time to review your policy and make the changes that truly reflect your values, incorporate relational practice and empower your staff to take ownership of behaviour management.

Try this

If you are a school leader, use the following lines of enquiry to help review your policy:

- Is the content of the behaviour policy an appropriate balance between positive behaviour strands and consequences and/or sanctions? Where is the emphasis?

- Are there references to SEND, attachment and adverse childhood experiences (ACEs)? Is the policy trauma-aware?

- How much focus is there on fixed-term and permanent exclusions?

- How are detentions used?

- Does the policy really represent the values and ethos of the school?

- Does the policy include support and intervention?

- Is behaviour improving over time, therefore indicating a successful policy?

- Has the behaviour policy been reviewed and changed in light of more recent understanding about children's needs?

- Is there a graduated response to dealing with challenging behaviour?

- Is the SENDCO active in the delivery, monitoring and implementation of the school's behaviour policy?

- Are behaviour incidents reducing over time?

- Is the use of sanctions decreasing over time?

- If detentions are used, do they work? What evidence is there to suggest this?

- What are the patterns of fixed-term exclusions and what are they used for?

- Is appropriate reintegration practice used following fixed-term exclusions or isolation?

- What is the level of permanent exclusion and is this reducing?

- What is the profile of excluded pupils?

- What is attendance and persistent absence like?

- What is the impact of fixed-term exclusions on attendance?

- Is there any evidence of cohort change linked to off-rolling, in-year pupil movements, elective home education (EHE), or use of AP and/or PRU managed moves?

- What is the pastoral and behavioural staffing structure?

- What levels of expertise and training do specialist staff have?

- Is the emphasis of practice based on knowledge and understanding of trauma and attachment or is the practice sanction heavy, high control, no excuses?

- Does the school use restorative approaches?

- Does the school have any therapeutic input either formally or informally?

- Is behaviour data used to inform practice?

- Is behaviour management/support seen as part of SEND practice and acknowledged as such amongst staff?

- What third-party support is available in school?

- Are any specific behaviour interventions used?

- What training has been put in place for staff delivering interventions?

- What is the impact of these interventions?

- Are interventions focused on specific needs and linked to education, health and care plan (EHCP) outcomes or the assess, plan, do, review cycle?

- How much staff training and continuing professional development (CPD) is focused on behaviour?

- What whole-school behaviour training is in place?

- Is there an induction programme for new staff that is related to behaviour training?

- How are staff supported through post-incident supervision?

- Are pupils rewarded for positive behaviour and success?

- Is this a graduated approach that takes into consideration different starting points, context, pupils' backgrounds and so on?

- How is positive behaviour communicated to parents?

- How is the Key Stage 2 to Key Stage 3 transition managed for the most vulnerable?

- How does the school manage internal transitions, including class-to-class and year-to-year movements?

- What reasonable adjustments are made for children with behaviour-related SEND (SEMH needs)?

- If a pupil is known to have SEND, how is this monitored?

- Is there an 'assess, plan, do, review' process in place for pupils with SEMH needs (even if they do not have an EHCP)?

- Who is involved in and/or leads the construction of the behaviour policy?

■ Are staff involved in reviewing the behaviour policy?

■ Are pupils involved in reviewing the behaviour policy?

Policy in a pandemic

In March 2020 the UK was hit with the unparalleled challenge of dealing with a global pandemic. Educational settings adapted with amazing agility and learning continued in creative and innovative ways. With the virus came heightened anxiety, increased stress levels and exposure to trauma – for both staff and children. Schools in England were asked, by the Department for Education, to review their behaviour polices to incorporate strategies to deal with children's return to full-time education in light of their exposure to the national lockdown, ever-rising death rates and a 'new normal'. This highlighted the need to be more aware, in our schools, of the significance of anxiety and its impact on behaviour.

Astonishingly, some schools changed their behaviour policies in response to the government's directive by doubling down on their sanctions-driven approach. They added additional punishments related to rule breaking and assumed that they would need to be even harsher with their responses – a whole new level of zero tolerance. Some even responded by turning school halls into large socially distanced isolation rooms or increasing their use of fixed-term exclusions.

However, others concentrated on relational practice, incorporating more awareness and skill-building around working with children experiencing mental health problems, anxiety and trauma. They commissioned training for staff from relational experts and added therapeutic interventions to their armoury of support. They realised that children were experiencing previously unknown levels of anxiety, so there needed to be a focus on care, relationships and support in school. Many realised that this had been missing from their previous approach and were stimulated to change by the crisis.

Some schools did not need to change as their behaviour policies were already relational, and already included strategies for dealing with trauma and stress. They could easily be adapted to meet the demands and challenges emerging from the communities they serve. They already acknowledged anxiety-based behaviours and recognised that this is driven by emotions and feelings. The staff were well-trained for the new normal and needed very little adaptation.

Try this

If you are a principal or head teacher, replace your behaviour policy with a relationships policy – be brave and give it a go. You will be amazed at how a simple adjustment of the title will change the way it is perceived and the cultural impact it has. Obviously, you will have to change the content too if it is to truly be your new, disguised behaviour policy.

Rigour, routine and structure

I have always been of opinion that consistency is the last refuge of the unimaginative.

Oscar Wilde[2]

Whether training to be a teacher, completing a newly qualified teacher (NQT) programme or being inducted at a new school, we are constantly told that consistency is the panacea of all behaviour management. It is written about in books, talked about by 'experts' and used to underpin policy. As mentioned, the term consistency – if not fully understood and/or placed in the wrong context – can be hijacked to justify harsh punishments. It can be used to present a strong stance that does not consider any form of discretion. Without discretion we risk alienating children and not allowing them to feel understood. Consistency can therefore be used to justify zero-tolerance and no-excuses behaviour policies – 'we need to be

---

2 Oscar Wilde, The Relation of Dress to Art: A Note in Black and White on Mr. Whistler's Lecture, *Pall Mall Gazette* (28 February 1885). In Robert Ross (ed.) *Miscellanies by Oscar Wilde*, Project Gutenberg ebook edn. Available at: http://www.gutenberg.org/files/14062/14062-h/14062-h.htm.

consistent'. You've heard the expression about trying to fit a square peg into a round hole. If consistency is what we strive for, then we are constantly trying to get square pegs into round holes and expecting them to fit. If they do not fit, we force them until they break, or we throw them away and replace them with round ones.

We must ask ourselves if we believe that we should be consistent in other aspects of education. When looking at the teaching of English or maths, do we stick to the consistency rule or do we personalise and differentiate? When teaching science, do we consider prior attainment when planning lessons and setting work? It is expected of us, as educators, to fill gaps, sequence learning and allow opportunities for revisiting areas that are not secure. We are expected to notice developmental gaps in children's understanding and to assess their knowledge constantly. If we find that children are missing essential academic skills, it is required that we teach them the bits that are absent. When it comes to behaviour, surely we must also personalise our approach? We have an opportunity to differentiate the style, look at what does and does not work, and be forensic and sophisticated in how we plan for dealing with challenging behaviour – one size does not fit all.

Enquiry behaviour management

When developing behaviour policy in my schools, we adopt the process of 'enquiry behaviour management'. This is when we attempt to solve a behaviour problem through investigation and detailed enquiry. Doing this allows us to be solution focused – concentrating on finding the cause of a behaviour rather than punishing at the end point. When using an enquiry approach, it is important to investigate what a child might be feeling and why they may have responded in a certain way. This allows us to respond to the feelings the child may be experiencing and not just focus on the end behaviour. This may sound hard, but we developed a successful process of genuine enquiry and planning for mitigating challenging behaviour. This would often include the use of routine and structure, and high levels of organisation completed with rigour. We need to help children to stop falling over, rather than offering a large supply of plasters to stick on grazed knees.

The *Special Educational Needs and Disability Code of Practice* refers to the cyclical process of assess, plan, do and review.[3] The guidance highlights the importance of this four-part cycle to SEN support, but there is no reason why this cannot be considered when dealing with challenging behaviour. It is essentially a way to structure an enquiry approach that gives schools the framework for a graduated response to meeting the requirements of children with additional needs. The enquiry process includes assessing needs; planning how to meet these needs with consideration and sophistication; implementing the planning with accountability and responsibility; then reviewing the impact and measurable outcomes of the plan in order to change, develop or repeat a strategy or intervention.

Micro-structures

Primary teachers are exceptional at practising routines. It is something that is drilled into them during training and continued throughout their careers. It is from them that we should all learn and recognise the impact of routines on managing behaviour across all educational settings and phases. Routines allow children to know what to expect and therefore train them in how to do it. Their days are organised, structured and packed with routines linked to high expectations. In an SEMH setting we take this to the next level and introduce micro-structures. We consider, with forensic focus, almost every movement and transition a child will make in a school day – and plan for it. This is not consistency; it is rigour, routine and structure. This allows high expectations to be set and children can be reminded of standards and those expectations, as well as being encouraged and supported to follow structures. Consistency would mean everyone doing the same thing without context, consideration of ability or discretion, and with too much consistency we set some children up to fail. In some cases, a behaviour policy with too much emphasis on consistency will have to accept that there will be a degree of failure. Failure, in these schools, is an accepted side effect. Therefore, we often see

---

3 Department for Education and Department of Health, *Special Educational Needs and Disability Code of Practice: 0 to 25 Years: Statutory Guidance for Organisations Which Work with and Support Children and Young People Who Have Special Educational Needs or Disabilities.* Ref: DFE-00205-2013 (January 2015). Available at: https://assets.publishing. service.gov.uk/government/uploads/system/uploads/attachment_data/file/398815/SEND_ Code_of_Practice_January_2015.pdf.

high exclusion rates in schools with strict, no-excuses behaviour policies, in which the focus is on consistency.

Flexible consistency

By recognising that we need to adopt a graduated response, appreciate additional needs and consider that some children will not automatically 'fit', we begin the process of flexible consistency. 'Flexible consistency' is a term that I adopted many years ago when discussing how fragile the term 'consistency' is and how it can lead to justifying unreasonable and inappropriate sanctions. The term was, and remains, an oxymoron. I would have many discussions with members of staff who demanded that a child be punished for committing a rule infringement. Irrespective of the circumstances, the background, any contributing factors or the child's own individual needs, consistency justified the allocation of a punishment to an infringement. Consistency was used as a tool to insist on retribution – teachers wanted revenge. This behaviourist approach, with a focus on sanctions, was not working. Pupils were not given the opportunity to discuss incidents and so learn how to manage themselves and their emotions. We, as a school, were focusing on the symptoms not the cause, and the medicine that we administered was not working. Using flexible consistency was the first step on the journey away from a behaviourist approach and towards relational practice.

Flexible consistency allowed for personalisation and reasonable adjustments. It gave us a focus for sophisticated discussion that enabled rigour, high expectations and structure but without compromising responsibility. Staff began to look at things differently and reflect more on their own responses. They were able to be more enquiry focused and to look closely at individual needs. Staff began to be problem solvers, looking for solutions, not revenge. This approach also allowed us to be true to our values, without compromise. Flexible consistency became an integral part of our practice and was even written into the behaviour policy. To this day it is used to frame training and allows staff to understand the importance of personalisation.

Sally arrived in my Year 11 geography class without her homework. She was a lovely, hard-working, diligent girl. She concentrated hard in class and never usually missed deadlines. She really wanted to achieve that magical GCSE C grade, but was a classic borderline pupil. She lived on the council estate close to the school and experienced chaos both in her family and in the community. Daily life was a struggle for her, but she managed it exceptionally well. The school had a simple homework policy – and who was I to disagree with it? If a child did not hand their homework in on time, then they received an automatic thirty-minute detention after school – no excuses. When I asked Sally why she had not done her homework she gave me an excuse to consider: 'I was trying to do my homework but there was a car burning on the road outside the house, so I couldn't concentrate.'

Consistency dictates that Sally receives a thirty-minute detention, irrespective of how she may have been feeling as the car was burning outside her house. The 'rule' did not consider the anxiety or stress associated with an incident that many of us would find stressful. How would you feel if you were trying to concentrate on a piece of work whilst a car burned on the street outside your house? Behaviour policy mandates that there are no excuses acceptable for missing homework deadlines. That was twenty years ago, and I will leave it to you to decide what you think I did.

Rigour is required every day in schools. This is a far more appropriate word than 'consistency'. If structures and routines are in place, then all staff must be rigorous in their pursuit to maintain them. We may need to adjust and adapt them to suit the needs of individual children, but teachers need a determined sense of rigour to maintain the standards we expect. When working with challenging children, it is especially important to maintain routines and focus on those micro-structures. It is so easy to become complacent and relax the rigour. If routines and structures are not checked and monitored closely then they can fall away. When this happens, the children lose their focus.

Try this

■ If you are a leader with responsibility for behaviour management, try an enquiry approach. To do this you'll need a team of colleagues to help you. If you are trying to resolve a problem with Kyle, then you need to create 'Team Kyle'. Team Kyle will include as many adults as possible who work with him. If you feel this group may be too large, stick to the ones you know will make a positive contribution and be solution focused. It is essential that you try to include adults who have strong relationships with Kyle and some who do not. You should include your SENDCO too. Do not ignore or underestimate the contribution a great SENDCO can have on this enquiry process. When your team is together, you can interrogate everything you know about Kyle. Read his file and his reports, and talk about his home environment. You need to look at patterns of attainment, both current and prior, as well as his incident record. You will be able to see if there are patterns or correlations – maybe even spikes in behaviour incidents that you can start to associate with specific times of day, locations or peers. Now you can start to plan for managing behaviour, based on thorough enquiry and a forensic approach. You will be amazed at how quickly you see correlations and patterns and learn how colleagues deal with Kyle specific to his needs and context. Use flexible consistency to build support for him. Do not get bogged down in the details of your behaviour policy; put it to one side for now and concentrate on the enquiry process. Your enquiry can be based on the following question: 'How do we help Kyle to be successful at school?'

If you are a teacher, start to plan for managing behaviour. Include a section in your lesson plans that explicitly highlights how you are going to deal with challenging behaviour. Link this to the enquiry approach by looking for patterns and triggers that relate to certain children. Include any support staff or teaching assistants you may have in your planning – talk to them. Do not feel embarrassed if you are struggling with a certain pupil; accept it and plan your approach. Talk to your colleagues about how they manage that child. You will probably find that they are also struggling, and you can support each other. Give as much thought to planning for behaviour as you do the lesson content. Think carefully about the micro-structures in your classroom. This needs to include transitions in and out of the room; any movement for activities; use of equipment and resources; the lesson activities; interactions with peers; and seating arrangements. This is where you need to establish your routines and rules with children – you are setting your expectations. Children need to know, explicitly, what you expect them to do, so do not assume that they will know if you don't make it clear. You must be the one in charge in the classroom, and setting your routines and expectations makes that clear to everyone. This may be something as simple as making sure children line up at the door or that they know they should not move around the room without first seeking permission. This is not authoritarian; it is cooperative. Co-constructing your rules and routines with your class will get their buy-in. This level of planning will give you the reminders and prompts you may need. Also, remember to review your lesson afterwards. Ask yourself what went well and what did not work.

Learning from your Carls

As an NQT I used to dread Thursdays. I would wake up in the morning in a cold sweat and with a sense of dread associated with five back-to-back Year 9 geography classes. I still hold a deep grudge against whoever constructed that timetable and exposed me, a mere NQT, to what can only be described as geographical torture. The day would start off OK, but then go downhill fast – after about the first fifteen minutes. As the bell sounded at the end of the day, I would be reconsidering my career choice on a weekly basis. At that time, I had no options available to me other than to muddle through, reflect, plan, weep and dust myself off to start it all again the following week. I had no system to help me, no person to call on and no button to press to have children removed. After the door closed behind the thirtieth pupil, I was left alone with them for an hour. Then another hour with the next class, then another hour with the next, then a brew and a cry, then another hour and another class, then a final hour with the final group.

This was the time in my career when I truly realised the power of relationships and making connections. I needed to connect emotionally with these children, particularly the big hairy lads who used to run around on the tables and throw things at each other and me. I clearly remember Carl, who once asked me for a fight after school – I declined his kind offer. Carl was the reason I could never sleep on a Wednesday night.

Thanks to Thursdays I learnt the importance of making those strong, emotional relationships with pupils. I took the friendly, kind and supportive approach, despite advice from colleagues to adopt strict sanctions and follow the detention policy. I did my own version of enquiry behaviour management – although at the time I did not realise it. I thought about and considered Carl. I realised that in the five classes that I taught on Thursdays (so about 150 children in total), only ten children were causing me anxiety. I was being overwhelmed and seeing nothing but the negatives. I needed to redress the balance. I talked to colleagues and found out about the lads and their contexts. I even went on a visit with the education welfare officer to the estate where they all lived. This really gave me a sense of the challenges that they faced. I made sure that my lessons developed their curiosity and I even pretended to support Barnsley Football Club. I met them at the door with a welcome smile, even though I was often terrified. I managed my classroom well, with routines and structures that considered the movement of the children. I planned for activities that I knew would not allow for disruption. I used rigour and structure in my lesson planning with a heightened consideration for each of those ten boys. I reflected after each lesson and changed and adapted my approach. I did not resort to detentions. It was physically exhausting and emotionally draining but I learnt so much. By the end of the school year things were easier but they were never easy.

Thursdays changed my career. They taught me that schools have many Carls, and that Carls need strong relationships, they respond well to routine and structure and need flexible consistency. At that time, I knew nothing about neuroscience or trauma; I just knew, instinctively, that Carl needed people to care about him and allow him to be accepted. Those Thursday classes did not need consistency in the form of sanctions, but they did need rigour, routine and high expectations.

I saw Carl fifteen years later in Barnsley Hospital Accident and Emergency Department. We laughed and chatted together as he sat in a wheelchair with his football kit on, nursing an injury and waiting for an X-ray. He had been to prison for a while for burglary but now had a family and was full of spirit (I remember his spirit very well from fifteen years before). Before he wheeled himself away down the corridor, he shook my hand, thanked me for not giving up on him and, in his words, apologised for being a 'little shit' at school. And although we were two adults having a conversation, he still referred to me as 'sir' throughout, which was lovely.

Do not think that you are a failure if you struggle with a difficult class. It happens to everyone and if they say otherwise then they are lying. If you have a Carl – or ten – roll up your sleeves, take an enquiry approach and consider the power of relationships and making positive connections.

Relational consistency is key

So, does consistency have a place in behaviour management? Of course it does, and this is mainly when we consider building trusting relationships and growing the connections we make with the children. It also means that we must have a consistent approach to how we work with our pupils, even if that is flexible. The EEF state clearly in their behaviour guidance that 'consistency is key'.[4] They also maintain that adults should know and understand their pupils and their influences, which aligns with a relational approach. Clearly consistency is a responsibility that the adults must carry when they are developing or sustaining relationships with pupils. Children need to trust and to be secure in those relationships. They need to know that this will not change and that you, as the caregiver, are consistent with the protection you offer through that strong emotional connection. You cannot afford to switch it on and off or you will lose it. We all have good days and bad days. We can arrive at work feeling anxious or grumpy. However, the children rely on us and the relational consistency we offer – especially those who do not get this elsewhere. That reliance puts great pressure on us and is a responsibility that we cannot take lightly. Therefore, our behaviour and responses need to be the consistent factor in the relationship. We must accept that the child is unlikely to be able to remain consistent and that they may challenge the bond you have with them. When you arrive at school, even if you are not feeling on top form, you must provide unconditional (consistent) positive regard, which includes managing and regulating your own mood.

Consistency is therefore a great word to use when associated with an adult's values and their attitude towards the children in their care. We need to give out a consistent message of positivity and fairness so that children know where they stand, which in turn provides the acceptance that the pupils need. Consistency comes with training and understanding, with all adults believing in the same approach and the school leadership committing to making it work. That is when we achieve the power of consistency.

---

4   Rhodes and Long, *Improving Behaviour in Schools*, p. 32.

Chapter Six

Intimacy, warmth, banter and trust (and a bit about the brain)

When positive relationships begin to thrive in a school, it comes alive. Adults and children are happy and comfortable in the building. They know and understand what the expectations are and work together to achieve them. This is true even in the toughest of schools. If the adults embrace the philosophy and values of the school, then the tone is set. Adult behaviour can now begin to strongly influence the behaviour of the children.

Try this

■ If you are a school leader, meet and greet the pupils every morning at the front gate or door. Make every child's first interaction with school positive every day. Do not use this time to correct uniform or point out the child with the wrong coloured socks. Give every child a warm greeting and mean it. Include this in your behaviour policy: that pupils are greeted warmly and positively by adults as they arrive in school. Make sure that you lead by example. Make sure that other adults are doing the same. This may seem basic, but use the children's names, ask them how they are, chat to them about things you know they enjoy. If all else fails, ask them about sport, music, TV or films. Do the same at the end of the day: make the end of the day as positive as it can be. Make sure the most vulnerable and challenging children get the most positive attention of all as their first interaction of the school day. Deal with the wonky tie later, or at least do it with good humour and warmth.

■ If you are a teacher, do the same at your classroom door. Stand at the door and welcome the children. Be positive, smile and laugh with them.

Do the same when they leave. See them off as you would with friends who have come to visit you at home.

- If you are an adult in a school, whatever your role, then engage children in positive conversation and chat as you move around the site. Ask them questions that are nothing to do with schoolwork. Say hello and ask them how they are doing. Think about how you appear to them. Are you smiling and buoyant or are you miserable and grumpy? Your every interaction has an impact on the tone of the day. You will have hundreds of interactions every day and each one of them counts. Yes, you work hard and you need a break but try having your lunch with the kids first. Sit with them and chat to them as you would with your own family. Time spent like this will build strong relationships and make emotional connections. The benefits of this simple interaction are immeasurable.

Banter

Banter is often misunderstood and can be thought to be somewhat inappropriate for school. Banter in this case is quite simply a friendly and warm interaction between adults and children, but also between adults. As adults move around school or engage with their peers in the company of pupils, they are modelling behaviour constantly. They are setting the tone. Therefore, appropriate banter is extremely powerful. Chatting to children in a friendly and fun way puts them at ease and strengthens relationships and respect. It helps children to feel secure and accepted, allowing them to feel understood and develop self-esteem. Self-esteem is the gateway to being confident. This is the power of banter. Effective banter should never leave a child feeling upset, ridiculed or humiliated. It should be warm and fun, never sarcastic and never patronising. If banter is anything but a positive and warm interaction, then it certainly is not banter.

Banter leads to warmth and a sense of intimacy. Children begin to trust adults and believe that they care. Adults will develop their own belief in the children too, understanding them and learning their personalities. This leads the way to authentic care. Authentic care is only achieved if the adults believe in the children and the children believe that the adults believe in them.

Relationships and the brain

The development of intimacy, warmth, banter and trust can be justified by understanding the limbic brain, the part where we make choices about social and emotional interactions. Consultant paediatric neurologist Dr Andrew Curran explains how neuroscience gives us a reason and a rationale to get relationships right. Managing the amount of dopamine (a critical chemical in the brain that makes it run normally and an essential neurochemical for learning and attention) and the amount of serotonin (which contributes to our happiness and well-being) in our brains is crucial. The ratio of dopamine to serotonin must be right – they need to balance. Stress will flood our brains with dopamine and make it less functional – causing an unwanted imbalance, and this can lead to high-risk decisions and poor judgement. This is particularly the case in adolescence, during the onset of puberty, when the brain produces a burst of dopamine, causing this potential imbalance. So, dopamine, in the right concentrations and at the right time, allows us to deal with challenges and issues. The limbic brain controls most of the dopamine release and therefore we must be able to contribute to the control of the emotional limbic system.

Although this may appear simplistic, confidence enables a child to behave. In order to build confidence, they need self-esteem, and this derives from being understood and accepted. When a child is confident, they make an emotional connection that allows them to feel loved. If we can achieve all this, in sequence, then learning happens.

So, we can achieve learning in seven simple steps:[1]

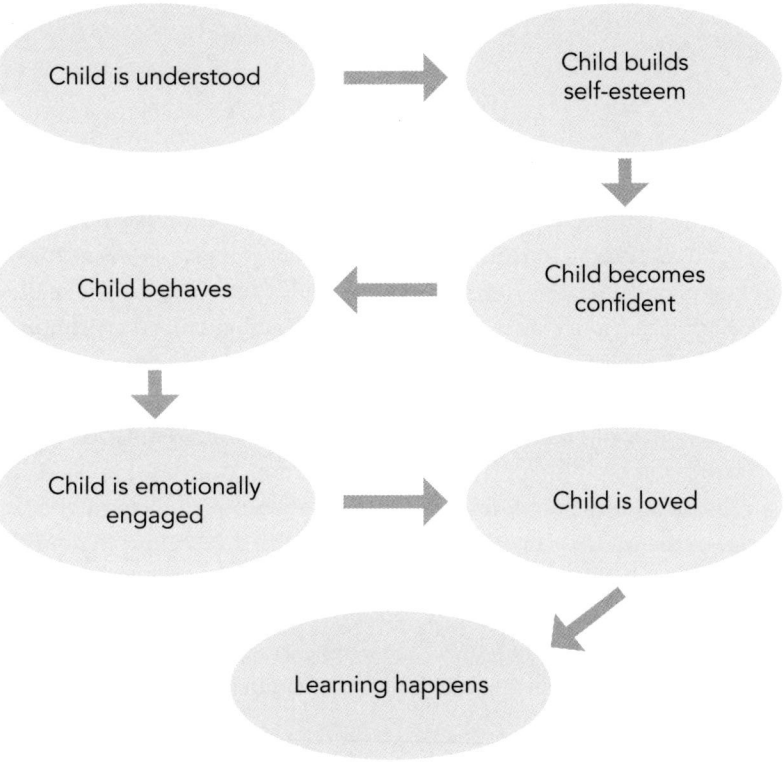

---

1   Adapted from the work of Dr Andrew Curran. Andrew, a paediatric neurologist and Independent Thinking Associate, delivered a day of staff training at my school. It was this training that changed the way I think and is probably the best training I have ever had. Staff say that this was the best INSET they have experienced and that it really allowed them to think differently about behaviour. An example of similar training can be seen here: https://vimeo.com/250809215.

The power of play

We must never think that we should remove laughter in order to achieve compliance. We need to be able to smile, laugh and have fun. Pressure on schools brought about by high-stakes accountability should not detract from the fact that play is an integral part of our work. Neuroscience helps us to understand this. Children will achieve dopamine release through playfulness. Our most challenging children will struggle to regulate their emotions and we can help them do this through organised and structured play. We must also remember that many of our most challenging pupils will not have 'playful' time at home. Therefore, positive, playful and happy time with adults is something that will have a significant impact on developing self-esteem and confidence.

For toddlers and young children, pretend play with adults helps to develop language, cognitive skills and emotional responses. Relational play – meaning the child plays with, or alongside, an adult – is well known as an effective pedagogical approach in early childhood education. We also know that some children struggle to communicate. Incorporating play into the normal routine of a school will allow children to develop stronger emotional connections with adults, enhance their self-esteem and reduce anxiety. Playing together, and with an adult, will also allow the children to accept losing in a controlled way – but, most of all, experience innocent, child-like fun.

Try this

▦ If you are a school leader, consider how play can be part of a school-wide strategy. Develop time for relational play; normal playtime is not enough. Treat play as a key area of development strategy and include it in your development plan. See it as an intervention with its impact being better behaviour and improved engagement.

▦ If you are a teacher, allow time for play in the routine of your day. This can be part of a form time activity (maybe during registration period), with children encouraged to play together and with adults. You might offer a simple board game that can be completed over several days. It might also be appropriate to finish the day with 'organised play' before the pupils go home. It could even be that you provide play opportunities at break or lunchtime in the same way as colleagues might run clubs for sport or the arts. Encourage the most vulnerable pupils to take part.

Some of the most rewarding time I have spent with pupils has been when playing together. As adults, making time in the day to share play with pupils is rewarding and contributes greatly to improved relationships and therefore behaviour. I have spent hours kicking a football around with children at lunchtimes or playing board games in classrooms during breaks – developing relationships through warm and focused conversation with pupils. These interactions are essentially interventions: they allow time for you to learn about pupils, invest in them and build trust. This investment is then 'cashed in' when dealing with an incident or teaching a challenging class.

I can recall spending time in a Year 7 class playing with water and sand like you might see in an early years setting. The teacher had set up 'play stations' (not the video game kind) in the class to start the day. This included the sand and water activities as well as board games and craft challenges. The children were enthralled. I spent time pouring water from cups, down funnels and into bottles, laughing and smiling with the children and just having fun together. It was amazing to see 12-year-olds playing like they were four years old. These children were relishing playing with adults – something that some of them had never done at home. What was happening in that class at that moment was magical. This had been thoughtfully created as an intervention by the teacher; it worked.

I often recall fondly the time and effort spent by a higher level teaching assistant (HLTA) who taught his Year 11 group how to play strategic board games such as Warhammer and Risk. These children, who all had a reputation for presenting serious behaviour challenges, played calmly and without incident. They developed social skills, improved their concentration and had fun in a controlled, mature environment. That HLTA became a trusted adult who built strong emotional connections with those children and was able to manage their behaviour with skill and confidence. He knew them well, understood them and was able to work with them to resolve emotional and social problems. He was a stress reducer.

Understanding simple concepts from neuroscience, without baffling or over-whelming ourselves, helps us to look at how we can understand the behaviour of children and start to support them. It does not mean they have an excuse; they just have a reason.

Polyvagal theory and playfulness, acceptance, curiosity and empathy (PACE)

I have spent many years working in schools, and I have seen the benefit of play-fulness and linking acceptance and empathy to a school culture centred on the concept of unconditional positive regard. Therefore, it was encouraging to read and discover that I had been doing something that accidentally aligns with another theory.

Louise Bombèr and Daniel Hughes highlight the importance of schools consid-ering PACE when working with troubled children.[2] They also refer to the work of neuropsychologist Stephen Porges, and particularly his focus on how crucial the autonomic nervous system is in understanding arousal levels in children and their impact on behaviour.[3]

The polyvagal theory explores the concept of arousal levels associated with the sympathetic and parasympathetic branches of the autonomic nervous system (auto-matic vagal responses are linked to the stimulation of the vagus nerve). It suggests that sympathetic behaviours are associated with increased arousal and mobilisa-tion, whereas parasympathetic behaviours are associated with reduced arousal and immobilisation. Porges explains that when a child is under great stress, their response is either one of immobilisation, with a high pain threshold and the basic instinct of preparation for death, or of increased mobilisation, which leads to a

---

2   Louise Bombèr and Daniel Hughes, *Settling Troubled Pupils to Learn: Why Relationships Matter in School* (London: Worth Publishing, 2013).
3   Stephen W. Porges, *The Polyvagal Theory: Neurophysiological Foundations of Emotions, Attachment, Communication, and Self-Regulation* (New York: W. W. Norton, 2011).

fight-or-flight response. Both responses are all about self-protection. Parasympathetic responses include shame, dissociation and a feeling of helplessness, whereas sympathetic responses are more likely to involve rage, anger, panic and fear.

Both these responses occur when a child does not feel safe. Here, Porges introduces the concept of a third state that employs the brain's social engagement system. This allows communication and understanding, but only when they feel safe. This helps us to understand why pupils need to feel safe and not threatened at school. It also highlights how we need to respond when a child is stressed and unable to socially engage or communicate. The challenge we have, when managing behaviour, is to not perceive stress responses as children simply being 'naughty'. We must avoid resorting to the default behaviourist approach of using sanctions for what we misunderstand as children 'choosing' to misbehave.

It is common to hear adults accusing pupils of making poor choices or choosing to behave in a certain way. The polyvagal theory helps us to understand that a child's response may not be a choice but a neurological reaction and something that they cannot control. They may appear to be making a choice, but that is not necessarily the case. If they are reacting to stress or anxiety, then their agency is essentially taken away.

In my early teaching career, I would often link behaviour to 'choice' and therefore allocate blame; I knew no other way. Blame would then lead to a sense of requiring revenge and therefore a sanction would seem necessary. That was before I understood more about children's brains and had been shown how to look at things differently, assess them in a different way and respond accordingly. If, as teachers, we see all behaviour as children's choices, then we automatically default to a punishment mindset rather than attempting to understand why the child behaved in that way. The aim, for us, is to understand why the behaviour took place – what underlying needs there might be – and to address that rather than focus on the behaviour alone.

Many school behaviour policies assume that misbehaviour is a choice. We cannot assume that children will make the connection between cause and effect by threatening them with ever-escalating forms of punishment. If we base our behaviour policy on this, then we naturally employ a system that seeks to punish. It is important to stress, once again, that understanding behaviour rather than punishing it does not mean that we ignore or do not challenge. Expectations can, and do, remain high even if 'control' is not predicated on the use of sanctions. We must therefore examine our own behaviour, the systems we have in school and the ways in which they are deployed. We must ask ourselves whether we provide an emotionally safe space for children, particularly those who are already experiencing stressful lives and who live in challenging environments.

Providing an emotional safe space for children means that we must embrace a level of acceptance, and this needs to be communicated by adults through their inter-actions. Every child is different, and we must accept them for who they are; we must not be preoccupied with changing them into someone else. The start of the school day is a good example of how acceptance begins, as children need to feel wel-comed and safe. Your language needs to portray acceptance in order to gain trust. Remember Faye? She needed to know that the adults at school were not going to reject her. She needed to know that she mattered and was accepted. Every morning this acceptance was reaffirmed through a warm greeting. She was trying to push the adults away by swearing at them, but the adults did not go anywhere. She was testing their commitment and authenticity and found that she was welcomed in a space that eventually felt safe. She therefore allowed herself to be accepted. Too many schools, and the adults in them, fail to provide acceptance and are focused on changing pupils through immediate compliance. If compliance is not instant, then the child falls into the punishment system and is likely to eventually be excluded. They are essentially emotionally excluded on day one. In this sense, the children are expected to change to fit the school; they cannot expect to be accepted as they are. If a child feels accepted, however, they are far more likely to make the emotional connections with us that we need in order to be able to influence any change in their behaviour.

Curiosity and empathy

Your own curiosity and desire to understand a child's behaviour helps to generate acceptance and put children at ease. Without being confrontational, adults can simply be curious and show this in the language that they use to help children reflect. The challenge is to allow yourself to be curious rather than reactionary. Curiosity, by allowing your questions to stimulate a pupil's response and make them feel at ease, helps you to tackle and address an incident. If you are curious then you are automatically being non-judgemental. If you can be non-judgemental then you will allow a child to remain engaged with you and they are therefore less likely to escalate their response and become more distressed. Your use of language, your behaviour and your approach once again becomes the key to manging behaviour. In Chapter Eight we will look at the use of language and how effective it is in the management of challenging behaviour.

It is entirely appropriate to also consider the children's own curiosity and their approach to learning. When I first worked with children with SEMH needs we focused on engaging teaching as the key to successful learning. It was the number one school improvement priority: the behaviour policy was essentially the teaching and learning policy. It was based on the understanding that if the children made an emotional connection with the teacher, and their curiosity was stimulated, then the experience of learning would be enjoyable. I would show visiting colleagues around the school and we would see curious children who were emotionally engaged with teachers and behaving themselves. When we were asked about the behaviour policy and its content, although we had one, our response would always start with discussing the teaching and learning policy.

I remember sitting in a series of Year 11 GCSE physics lessons and seeing the emotional bond the teacher had created with the children. The subject was irrelevant, but the person was everything. He had allowed them into his world, given them enough of himself as a person to build such a strong relationship that they wanted to learn for him. They were permanently curious and therefore perfectly behaved. This group were all excluded from mainstream education – children with extreme behaviour and troubled backgrounds. They loved physics because they loved the teacher, and the teacher loved them back. They all passed their physics GCSE.

Curiosity will therefore stimulate learning and make it more enjoyable and effective. This will lead to a dopamine release that will make the child feel good about learning, causing them to engage and therefore behave. This may seem simplistic and unrealistic, but it is all about context. There is no magic spell that says that a focus on curiosity will solve all behaviour issues – of course not. But it is something that must be considered as part of the overall approach to behaviour management. We regularly hear the term 'make your lessons worth behaving for', but this is often criticised. Some believe that this is an unacceptable expectation and that children should – nay, must – behave irrespective of the quality, style or content of the lesson. That said, as a committed and passionate teacher, why would you not try your best to generate curiosity and engagement in your lessons? Why would you just expect and assume that a child will behave? Why wouldn't you accept that as a professional you have a responsibility to engage your pupils' curiosity and create an emotional bond with them?

One way to engage pupils and to generate curiosity is to make them 'learn accidentally' – and this can be achieved through a great, engaging curriculum. I was lucky to work with two great professionals who developed a fantastic curriculum based on the use of creative pedagogy to explicitly engage challenging children. My vice principal at the time at Springwell Community Special School, Verity Watts, worked with a great friend and colleague of mine, Hywel Roberts,[4] to develop our Elements Curriculum – with a lot of hard work from the teachers. It was this work in the classroom that had a significant impact on the children's behaviour: they were curious, they were engaged and they behaved.

In order to create the opportunity for curiosity, and therefore learning, first the child must feel safe. We must be careful with our language choices and mannerisms; being irritated and impatient, for example, will make a child's already stressed response worsen. A raised and angry voice will force a child to be defensive rather than reflective. Their priority, as a response to an angry interaction, will not be for effective and positive social communication. Children will also lie to attempt to stop whatever it is that is making them feel unsafe – without thinking it through or considering the consequences. To many children, lying is a defensive measure, learnt to protect them from punishment. If children are heavily and regularly punished, they will develop a technique to avoid it – lying. All teachers can recall incidents when they have asked for, or demanded, answers from pupils following an incident and the response has been a lie or blatant denial. If children feel threatened, then they will defend themselves – and one way to do this is through lying. If they trust you, they are far less likely to lie.

At this point empathy will also play its part. Empathy allows us to understand how a child must be feeling and to place ourselves in that situation. We can challenge behaviour and expect certain standards, but it is how we do it that is important.

---

4   Hywel did a great deal of development work with teachers to adapt their pedagogical approach to embrace the arts. Lots of examples and insights can be found in his book: Hywel Roberts, *Oops! Helping Children Learn Accidentally* (Carmarthen: Independent Thinking Press, 2012).

Even adults can be defensive when confronted. We can respond angrily to what we believe is a provocative challenge. When driving, if you bump into the back of the car in front of you at a roundabout, then you know the accident is your fault – the law says so (you have broken the rules). If the driver of the other car steps out, shaking their fist and shouting angrily, then you will automatically respond in a stressed way – anyone would. You might have a parasympathetic response and freeze – unable to communicate. Your sympathetic nervous system might take over and so you respond with a fight response – shouting back and matching their aggression. The situation may escalate, tempers may rise and others, including the police, may need to intervene.

If the driver of the other car emerges quietly and calmly with an understanding wave and compassionate shrug of the shoulders, then our response will be entirely different. In this case we will be able to communicate: we will feel safe enough to discuss the accident. We are likely to accept responsibility, apologise (genuinely) and exchange insurance details. The situation is resolved, relationships are intact, and your no-claims bonus is the only thing that takes a hit.

Imagine, then, that the driver of the other car is the teacher and you are the child. You have done something wrong and broken a rule. The response of the teacher (the injured party) can take one of two approaches, of which they are in control. They could show calm and empathy, whilst still understanding that a rule was broken. Conversely, they could show anger and aggression because a rule was broken, and you should know better. The approach from the adult, and their ability to regulate their response, leads to two potentially very different reactions from the child.

During my NQT year I was involved in an incident involving a fight between two Year 10 boys – something that I had no experience of dealing with because, after all, I was only a month or so into my first teaching job. They certainly did not cover breaking up fights on my PGCE course at the University of Sheffield. It was a gloomy Friday afternoon – typical weather for November in Yorkshire. In those days we had afternoon breaks (not many secondary schools have afternoon breaks anymore as it's considered too dangerous). NQTs were allocated the playground duty slots nobody else wanted, and on Friday afternoons the other teachers needed to rest after going to the pub at lunchtime. I was with a more experienced colleague who took one boy away as I dealt with the other. Even with my inexperience I could see that the boy was full of adrenaline – shaking, out of breath and red faced. The fight had lasted a matter of seconds yet had generated a crowd of what seemed like a thousand screaming teenagers and was developing into something like a scene from *Gladiator*.[5] Lee, the boy who I had taken aside, could not communicate – that was clear. He was incapable of an appropriate emotional response or any form of rational behaviour. My priority, assessed through nothing more than instinct, was to reassure him and steer him away from the screaming crowd. I did this with a soft hand on his shoulder and a quiet but assertive whisper.

My colleague, dealing with Mackenzie, had taken a different approach. I could see his finger wagging, his body language was aggressive and he was visibly angry. He was challenging Mackenzie, standing up close in his personal space and forcing him to back away. Mackenzie, like Lee, was full of adrenaline, shaking and incapable of rational or controlled behaviour. He had an adult shouting and pointing at him, moving towards him and forcing him backwards. It was too much for Mackenzie, and his limbic system took over. I turned just in time to see Mackenzie punch my colleague in the face. I now had to deal with Mackenzie too, as the baying crowd erupted as if Maximus had just won a battle in the colosseum. Luckily, being an NQT, I was able to immediately hand over the 'problem' to the head of year – a luxury enjoyed by teachers new to the profession.

Mackenzie was permanently excluded that day and never returned to school. He was sent to a PRU and some years later found himself in the criminal justice system. Mackenzie was from a troubled background. He had clearly experienced significant trauma in his childhood, and he needed repair and support rather than punishment and rejection. This was another career-defining moment for me – one I often reflect on. Could things have been different for Mackenzie with a different adult response to this incident? Of course, hitting a teacher is very serious, but fights amongst peers are, unfortunately, a common incident in secondary schools across the country.

Bruce Perry and Christine Dobson explain that children who have experienced trauma need to go through a process of repair known as the neurosequential model.[6] In its most simple terms, this means that we must try to repair the wounded

---

5   *Gladiator*, dir. Ridley Scott (2000).
6   Bruce D. Perry and Christine L. Dobson, The Neurosequential Model of Therapeutics. In
     Julian D. Ford and Christine A. Courtois (eds), *Treating Complex Traumatic Stress Disorders
     in Children and Adolescents, Scientific Foundations and Therapeutic Models* (New York: The
     Guilford Press, 2013), pp. 249–260.

brain from the brainstem upwards, building experiences as we go. To do this in a therapeutic situation would include an assessment and mapping exercise followed by focused therapeutic work. However, in a school environment we can still play our part. Dealing with challenging incidents, as adults in school, can be extremely difficult and sometimes it helps to follow a sequence to frame your response.

Try this

If you are dealing with a behaviour incident, try to think about these three steps:

1. **Regulate:** This is the important first step of remaining calm and regulating your own response in order to make the child feel safe and not threatened by you. If the child is scared in that first exchange, then it will be difficult to move on without further escalation. It can be advantageous to give a child physical space and to not follow or chase them as they try to self-regulate. You must allow them into your calm rather than join them in their chaos. Your own regulation sets the immediate tone for dealing with the incident. Think of this initial phase as co-regulation – you are in it together.

2. **Relate:** This is the step when you empathise with the child, their situation and the response that they have had. If you know the child well and have a strong relationship with them, this will feel easier. If you do not have an existing relationship, then your skill is to make a quick and calm assessment of the situation and allow reflection time.

3. **Repair:** They now need to put things right, but, of course, they will need your help with this. You must resist imposing an immediate sanction and instead focus on reflection and discussion. The pupil may need your emotional support during the repair step. If you offer to help them to find a solution to their problem, then you start to build the safe emotional connection they require to put things right.

The window of tolerance and states of arousal

You will come across children whose behaviour presents as hyperactive and those who seem subdued or withdrawn. Both hyper and hypo states of arousal need to be understood before being addressed through relational behaviour management. Dr Daniel Siegel introduced the term 'window of tolerance', which is commonly used to describe our comfort zone or optimal arousal level.[7] We all fluctuate within this zone and sometimes fall out of the bottom (hypo) or burst through the top (hyper). In the hyper state, children may feel angry, overwhelmed or panicked. They may feel unsafe and hypervigilant, with racing thoughts. They could have a chaotic response or an emotional outburst – sometimes aggressive. Children in the hypo state will have no energy and may feel ashamed, disconnected or depressed. Think about these behaviours and how common they are amongst your pupils. Relationships are easy to manage and develop when children are in their window of tolerance but difficult when they are not. The limbic brain is once again taking over with fight-or-flight responses (hyper) and/or freeze responses (hypo).

Children who operate outside of their window of tolerance may need help to regulate and return to their comfort zone. Most of us will experience these fluctuations ourselves and are able to self-regulate. This is a learnt response that will have been developed over years and helped by protective caregivers during childhood. Without that early support, some children will struggle to self-regulate and will therefore need support from adults in school. Children who have experienced trauma may have a narrow comfort zone and we need to be prepared to help expand their window of tolerance or at least help them return to their calm state of arousal.

A common mistake in managing behaviour, and one that I am guilty of making myself, is to up-regulate a child who is already in a state of hyperarousal. This means we might believe that a child needs to 'burn off some energy', so we encourage physical activity thinking that it will tire them out. What we are actually doing is taking a child who is hyperaroused and making them even more hyperaroused. What we really should be doing is trying to calm them down so that they can return to their comfort zone.

---

7 Daniel J. Siegel, *The Developing Mind: How Relationships and the Brain Interact to Shape Who We Are* (New York: Guilford Press, 2002).

Children who are hyperaroused will need sensory intervention to calm down, and those who are hypoaroused will need sensory intervention to become more alert. If you feel that you are working with children who fall into these categories, then it would be a good idea to talk to your SENDCO about the use of a qualified occupational therapist. Occupational therapists are underused in schools and can add a whole new dimension to behaviour management by providing advice on sensory activities. This type of therapy can give instant, positive results that can help to stretch the window of tolerance and have long-lasting effects. Sensory activities can allow children to tolerate sensations and situations that they find challenging. They can also reduce unwanted sensory-seeking or sensory-avoiding behaviour – you are legitimately providing a sensory hit that they would otherwise seek elsewhere. Sensory activities can also regulate emotions and increase attention span by allowing children to remain in their comfort zone for longer periods of time.[8]

For children, regulation will often come from a loving parent or caregiver soothing them with a calm response, a hug or a cuddle, for example. The pressure of repetitive, rhythmic touch is automatically soothing. This is co-regulation and something we should attempt to replicate if we can – adults regulating 'with' children. It is important that schools seek professional advice from occupational therapists, but it is worth knowing about and understanding some of the techniques that have been successfully used in schools, after following professional advice:

▪ **Proprioception** (perception or awareness of the position of the body) can be achieved by lifting, pushing or pulling heavy objects. There may be an opportunity to ask the child to do a job that involves lifting, pushing or carrying something. It may be that you allow the child to dangle or swing from monkey bars or a climbing frame. Proprioception can be achieved through carrying a heavy rucksack or doing press-ups. Yoga can be effective, as can using a trampoline or a body sock.[9]

---

8   These ideas are based on sensory integration theory and sensory processing disorder. This short blog gives an overview of the work of Dr Lucy Miller and Dr Jean Ayres: GriffinOT, Sensory Integration Theory vs Sensory Processing Disorder What's the Difference? (27 December 2019). Available at: https://www.griffinot.com/sensory-integration-sensory-processing/.

9   Body socks are made of stretchy fabric such as Lycra. A child can climb inside them to get an all-over deep pressure sensory experience – a proprioceptive and tactile intervention. They are available as a specialist intervention item for schools to purchase.

- **Vestibular** (sense of balance associated with the inner ear) interventions will be anything that involves spinning or swinging – or even hanging upside down. Cartwheels, playing on playground swings and dancing are all useful vestibular interventions.

- **Tactile** (sense of touch) interventions involve light touch, deep pressure massage, messy play activities and play dough. Younger children will respond to dressing up or trying hot and cold foods. Playing in sand or dirt or working in the school garden will also act as a tactile intervention. The well-managed use of fidget toys will also help.

- **Auditory** (sense of hearing) interventions can simply involve listening to live or recorded music or natural sounds. Waves, rainfall or bird song can be powerful. Specialist calming music can be played softly in the background in classrooms and shared areas of the school, giving an extra calming influence throughout the day. Binaural beats – which occur when the brain processes two sounds that are at different frequencies at once – are ideal for meditation and calming.

- **Visual** interventions can simply involve the use of colour for calming or stimulating attention. It may be that in the classroom a teacher needs to be aware of any 'visual clutter' that can be distracting and to consider solid walls in neutral, soft colours. Teachers can also be conscious of where a child sits in the classroom to avoid visual distractions. In many classrooms, teachers will sit the most challenging children at the front of the class, but here they may be constantly turning around to seek visual stimulation. It may be easier to sit them at the back of the classroom where they can see everyone. You may wish to use visual timers for activities or even allow children to wear sunglasses. Lava lamps can be a good addition to a classroom or a calming space for children who require visual interventions.

- **Olfactory** (sense of smell) interventions can simply involve removing odours that may upset children and being aware of those that overstimulate. Certain smells can be calming and therefore may soothe or even stimulate children. Try scented play dough or an essential oils diffuser.

- **Taste** interventions link strongly with smell. Strong tastes can be used in games and to stimulate a child who is withdrawn. Mints, sour sweets or other strong-tasting foods can help to stimulate an under-sensitive child. However, always be aware of any food allergies, intolerances, or cultural and religious implications before using any food as an intervention.

These are just examples of how sensory activities can be used to help manage behaviour. It is important that we use experts when planning these kinds of interventions. Occupational therapists will be able to make suggestions and help plan activities for whole classes and individual children. Hopefully, these examples will give you some idea of how easy it can be to use a variety of activities to stretch a child's window of tolerance and/or help them return to their comfort zone.

This takes us back to the importance of fun, laughter and playfulness. The body needs oxytocin. This is the hormone that helps to counter the impact of too much cortisol (the stress hormone) and is released when we laugh and have fun. We must be mindful of not adding more stress to those who are already experiencing excessive and constant pressure. We must always be aware of our pupils' starting stress levels in the same way as we would consider prior attainment when planning academic work. It is within our means to provide opportunities for oxytocin release and cortisol control as best we can. Our aim is to know our pupils well, develop their resilience and maintain a healthy balance – all of this whilst delivering a curriculum; supporting social and emotional growth; making academic assessments; planning lessons; marking and assessing; ensuring safeguarding procedures are in place; protecting well-being; providing SEND support; personalising and differentiating appropriately; being mindful of British Values; and preparing for the scrutiny of Ofsted, learning walks and lesson observations. Is it any wonder that we need to give thought to managing both our stress levels and those of the children?

Chapter Seven

Background influences
(and a bit more about the brain)

The circle of influence

The circle of influence (see page 80) is a model developed by David Moore[1] as part of the National Programme for Specialist Leaders of Behaviour and Attendance (NPSLBA). This training programme was produced by the Department for Children, Schools and Families in 2007 for leaders of inclusion and behaviour. Aspects of the content, including this model, remain as important and relevant today as they were then.

A child is born into a circle of intimacy. Here they learn the behaviour that will forge the basis of their lifelong personality and disposition. They may be exposed to poverty and neglect. Swearing may be commonplace, and violence and aggression a part of everyday life. Here a child learns to behave based on their experiences and the activities of the people around them. They may be exposed to drug or alcohol abuse and, in some cases, be cared for by siblings not much older than themselves. There may be love and care in the home, but tainted by poverty and deprivation – a daily struggle to pay the bills and make ends meet. This brings with it stresses and strains on family life and parenting. A child may be born into a loving family, in which adults show unconditional love and support, and the child is provided for both emotionally and physically. Their development is supported by strong relationships with parents and/or caregivers who make sure that the children are fed, clothed and looked after appropriately in their formative years.

Children are then exposed to a circle of friendship. This includes trusted adults, such as close family friends, grandparents and neighbours. If these people are kind,

---

1   Adapted from a presentation given by David Moore. See David Moore, The Circle of Intimacy [video] (21 November 2011). Available at: https://www.youtube.com/watch?v=0A-iTNk0Cj4.

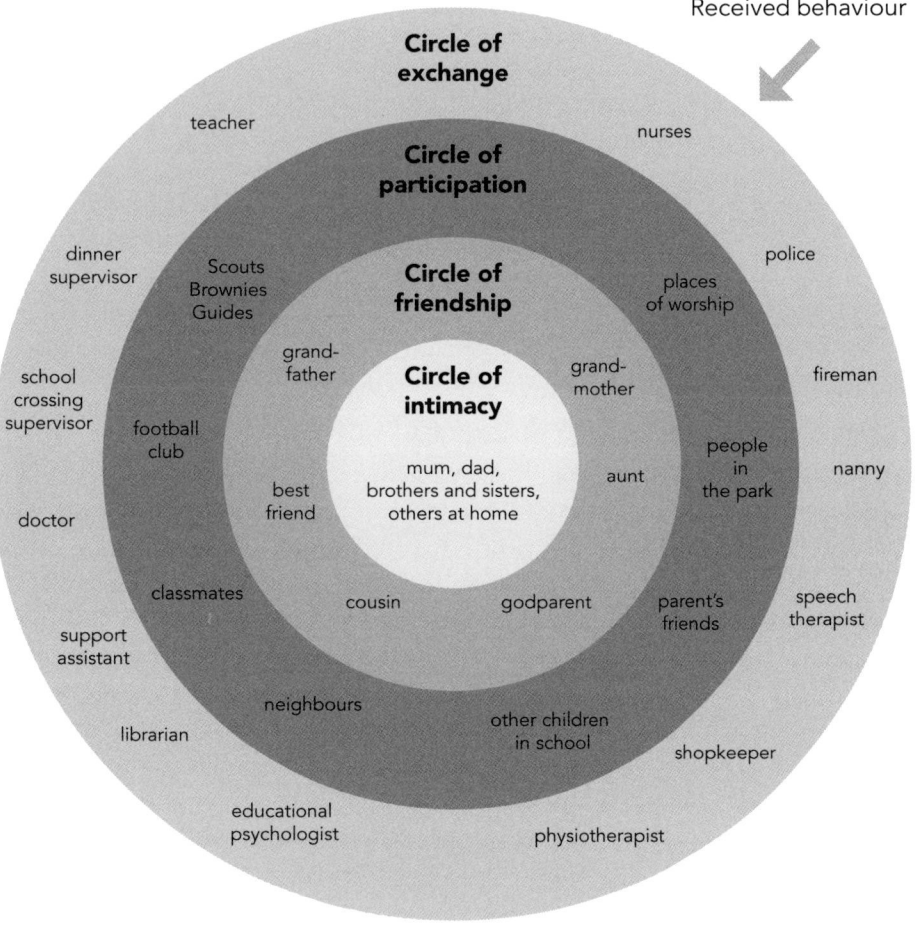

Received behaviour

The circle of influence

supportive and loving, they contribute a new and powerful learning experience. A child learns how to be with other people who care. Children learn so much from members of their 'extended family' (they don't have to be blood relations, of course), who show love and support in a different way to their parents or main caregivers. They also learn how to conspire – 'Here's some chocolate, Jonny. Don't tell your mum.'

I remember a lovely story about a friend's son, Tommy. He was playing the role of a shepherd in the school nativity play. With a tea towel on his head and 'Away in a Manger' fully rehearsed, he was ready for the production, which was taking place at the local church. Tommy's mum and dad, both being teachers, could not make it to the morning performance, so Great Aunty Pat had the proud honour of representing the family that day. She arrived early, before sunrise, in order to secure the front pew and sat there delighted, gushing with pride throughout the show. At the end of the performance the children were queuing in the aisle ready for their return to school. Tommy was within touching distance of Great Aunty Pat. She dipped into her handbag and produced a bar of chocolate which she quickly slipped into her great-nephew's hand. 'Thomas, that was wonderful,' she whispered. 'Here's a little present, but don't tell your teacher.' He had been told by his lovely aunty not to tell his teacher about the chocolate. He was immediately forced into a conspiracy and a cover-up.

That afternoon Tommy's mum arrived at school to collect him. He ran across the playground and embraced his mummy with a hug and immediately began to recall, with excitement, the morning's performance. He then explained how Great Aunty Pat had rewarded him with a chocolate bar, despite knowing that he was not allowed chocolate in school. When his mum asked what he had done with it, he cheekily placed his hand up his sleeve and revealed the prize that had been concealed inside his jumper all day. The chocolate was melted and deformed inside the wrapper but Tommy was happy as he ate it in the car on the way home. He had successfully conspired with his aunty against his teacher. He was five years old, he had chocolate and the world was good. These kinds of interactions are fundamental to behaviour development. However, imagine if you will, all the children who do not have a positive circle of friendship or who have no circle of friendship at all.

Now we introduce the circle of participation: the middle-class stronghold of behaviour development. This is where children participate in activities that allow them to develop and grow – Brownies, Scouts, football, netball, cricket, swimming, music lessons, and so on. They are exposed to authority, structure and rules. It takes real commitment from parents to support this phase of development. Swimming club can be five mornings a week at 6 am. This relies not only on parents' physical commitment to taking them but also on owning a car and having the ability to pay the fees. Local junior football clubs must pay for expensive kit, match fees and transport to fixtures. The costs may prove a barrier to participation. However, in this circle, children learn how to be with adults who have authority over them, and they develop relationships that will influence their personalities for the rest of their lives. We all know that some children simply do not have a circle of participation and therefore miss out on a significant and powerful developmental phase. But it is not their fault.

A circle of participation can prove to be a drain on finances. Historically, the working classes were heavily dependent on local sports teams, the church and the local working men's club for this area of development. The local club may no longer exist, participation in sports teams has become an expensive pastime and there has been a significant decline in church and other such community activities. All participation is reliant on willing and able adults for support and on the finances to pay for fees and equipment. It is easier now for a child to be confined to their electronic devices than to join a club. We also know that some children will disappear into their bedrooms for hours playing video games, and suchlike, meaning that they do not interact with adults and are not exposed to rules, structures or routines. They might return from school, get changed out of their uniform and disappear for hours before returning late at night – sometimes not returning at all.

Finally, we have the circle of exchange. Teachers, doctors and the police are all part of this group. Here children are exposed to adults who have authority over them in a formal sense. These are the people who are exposed to the behaviour that has already been learnt and embedded. If a child joins your school aged 11 and is unable to read, then we teach them to read. If they join the school and cannot behave appropriately, then what must we do?

Those children who move smoothly through the three previous circles access school almost entirely without concern. Those who have been exposed to a chaotic circle of intimacy often skip the next two developmental phases. The behaviour they have learnt – the 'received behaviour' – is what we see when they come into school; they have had no opportunities to intuit that different sorts of behaviours are expected of them in different relational contexts. Therefore, once again, we have choices to make – do we support the development of appropriate behaviours, with an understanding of context and empathy for their circumstances, or do we begin to punish the child by expecting them to change as a response to sanctions?

Try this

- If you are a school leader, share this model with every adult in the school. Allow them to understand the influences a child is exposed to and how this helps us to understand their behaviour. However, make sure that this is not seen as an excuse. Challenge the staff to think of ways to address deficits in social and behavioural development.

- If you are a teacher involved in an after-school club or lunchtime activity, focus on those children who do not have a circle of participation. If you get to know them really well, you will be able to identify the children who would not otherwise have these influences. Proactively encourage those who will benefit the most from being part of an extracurricular group. This may be hard as their default position will be not to attend. To many, it is easier not to be involved. They may need significant encouragement and support if they lack the confidence to participate in something new.

- If you are an adult in a school, whatever your role, ask to go out into the community your school serves. Drive around the catchment area with an attendance officer or a welfare officer. Request to join some home visits as a professional development opportunity in order to get a genuine understanding of the social and environmental challenges that some of the children face every day.

Adverse childhood experiences (ACEs)

There is another layer of complexity that sits within the circle of intimacy. This is the relatively new concept of ACEs.[2] It is now understood that children who are exposed to significant trauma in early life may suffer from cognitive impairment that can be seriously damaging to their long-term health if not addressed. We now understand the negative impact that stress hormones – such as cortisol and adrenaline – can have on the human body. We also know that these hormones, when released at an unusually high level by an expectant mother, can even begin to cause damage to an unborn child. ACEs can include all types of abuse and neglect, as well as parental mental illness, substance use, divorce, bereavement, incarceration and domestic violence. It is important to understand that exposure to ACEs does not automatically cause trauma and its associated long-term problems, but can be a significant contributing factor, dependent on each child's circumstances.

Knowing about the function and development of the brain can help us to understand behaviour; anything we understand better, we can deal with easier – both practically and emotionally. The work of Bruce Perry – an American psychiatrist and author – can help us to understand brain organisation and function and its links to behaviour. Put simply, the brain has three main functions:

1. Survive.

2. Mate.

3. Protect and nurture.

In order to complete these responsibilities, the brain has evolved thousands of interrelated functions and developed a hierarchy that starts with the lower brain (brainstem) and finishes in the upper brain (neocortex) – increasing in complexity as it goes. This hierarchy starts with the simpler physiological functions – such as heart rate, blood pressure, respiration and temperature regulation – and works through to more complex functions – such as language and abstract thinking.

---

2   Elizabeth A. Schilling, Robert H. Aseltine Jr and Susan Gore, Adverse Childhood Experiences and Mental Health in Young Adults: A Longitudinal Survey, *BMC Public Health*, 7(30) (2007). Available at: https://link.springer.com/article/10.1186/1471-2458-7-30.

Perry describes this as a 'neuroarcheological understanding of adverse childhood events'.[3] Each layer of the hierarchy reflects the experiences of a child's life, which can be either good or bad. This is our neurodevelopment and is directly linked to our behaviour:

> Our brain's complex structure is comprised of 100 billion neurons and ten times as many glial cells – all interconnected by trillions of synaptic connections – and communicating in a non-stop, ever-changing dynamic of neurochemical activity. The brain doesn't just pop into existence. This most complex of all biological systems in the known universe is a product of neurodevelopment – a long process orchestrating billions upon billions of complex chemical transactions. It is through these chemical actions that a human being is created.[4]

Disruption to the normal development of the brain, both environmental and genetic, can lead to abnormal neurodevelopment and therefore dysfunction. What we need to understand is that although changes in the brain take place throughout our lives, through neuroplasticity, the key stages of neurodevelopment take place in childhood. Both environment and genetics will affect it, and this introduces the nature versus nurture debate. However, we must understand that both play a part, and, put simply, genetic potential will not be realised without appropriate experiences. Neurodevelopment requires both nature and nurture.

A child's brain is vulnerable and more malleable to its environment than the adult brain. Extreme experiences, neglect and trauma in childhood can disrupt development. Symptoms of this disruption include sensory integration problems, hyperreactivity and poor regulation. These are the symptoms we often see played out in school in a child's behaviour.

A child's responses to exposure to ACEs is varied and dependent on age, history of previous experiences, predisposition to vulnerability and, importantly, the presence of a supportive and protective caregiver. If ACEs are prolonged and repeated,

---

3   Bruce D. Perry, The Neuroarcheology of Childhood Maltreatment: The Neurodevelopmental Costs of Adverse Childhood Events. In K. Franey, R. Geffner and R. Falconer (eds), *The Cost of Maltreatment: Who Pays? We All Do* (San Diego, CA: Family Violence and Sexual Assault Institute, 2001), pp. 15–37. Available at: https://divisionsbc.ca/sites/default/files/Divisions/Nanaimo/Neuroarcheology_2001_web.pdf, at p. 2.
4   Perry, The Neuroarcheology of Childhood Maltreatment, p. 2.

the child is more vulnerable. If the activation of stress hormones is sustained, symptoms may become severe and can reach the level of a clinical disorder. Attention deficit hyperactivity disorder (ADHD)[5] is an example of a condition in which children become hypervigilant and impulsive. This can be a result of having spent prolonged periods of time living in a low-level state of fear.

Attachment theory

You may well already be aware of attachment theory.[6] This is the emotional connection between two people that leads to a feeling of security. It is particularly relevant to the bond between a child and a caregiver (usually the mother) who provides food and care and responds sensitively and appropriately to the child's needs. It is suggested that children need to develop secure attachments in the first two to five years of their lives, and that if they do not do so then it may never happen. This primary attachment is important for the child's social development and is supported by attachments with other family members: their father, siblings, grandparents, etc. – those who form the circle of intimacy and the circle of friendship. We've already discussed how a lack of these positive close relationships can have a huge impact on children, and how their behaviour may be affected.

Disruption to the attachment between a child and their primary caregiver can cause long-term cognitive, social and emotional difficulties. Bowlby believed that this deprivation could lead to increased aggression, depression and affectionless psychopathy, meaning that the child would be unable to show warmth or concern

---

5   ADHD is a condition that affects children's behaviour and can make them restless. They may struggle with concentration and act on impulse. Inattentiveness can also be a symptom. Causes include genetics and brain function and structure deficiencies. Studies also suggest that people with ADHD may have an imbalance in the level of neurotransmitters in the brain or that those chemicals do not work properly. Other conditions are often related to ADHD, such as anxiety disorder, oppositional defiant disorder (ODD), conduct disorder, depression, sleep problems, epilepsy, Tourette's syndrome and dyslexia. Further information can be found at: https://www.nhs.uk/conditions/attention-deficit-hyperactivity-disorder-adhd/.
6   Attachment theory originates from the work of British psychologist John Bowlby, of which there are numerous interpretations. A good summary of Bowlby's work can be found here: Saul McLeod, Bowlby's Attachment Theory, *Simply Psychology* [blog] (5 February 2017). Available at: https://www.simplypsychology.org/bowlby.html.

towards others. They may act on impulse, show no remorse for wrongdoing and express themselves through anti-social behaviour.

The behaviour of the primary caregiver has a profound impact on the emotional development of the child:

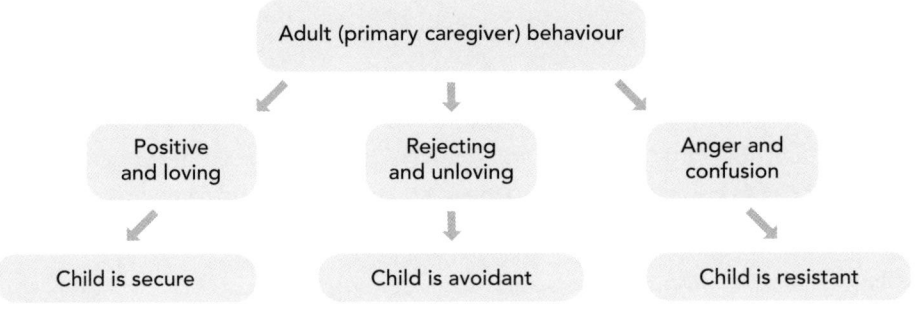

This presents just a snapshot of attachment theory, but the important thing to take from it is that, as relational practitioners, we can have a positive impact on children's behaviour if we endeavour to provide supportive and protective relationships. Serious attachment disorders can be supported by psychotherapy, and it is important that we seek professional advice and help when working with children with such conditions. However, it does help to understand why children may behave in certain ways and how their attachment history may have impacted on this. Knowing about attachment theory helps us to understand the power of positive relationships and of providing genuine love and support – helpful if we need to justify our relational approach and the strategies we employ.

Nurture approaches

Again, it must be emphasised that not all children who are exposed to traumatic events develop symptoms associated with ACEs. Familial and social circumstances play a fundamental role in protecting children. Supportive, calm, loving and nurturing caregivers can prevent symptoms from developing. Perry stresses that if a child is supported by a strong social fabric, they may develop their own healing process naturally by using the people around them.[7] If this is the case, forcing a child to attend therapy can be counterproductive and can expose traumatic memories.

Many schools now use nurture approaches to support children to develop their social and emotional skills. However, the term 'nurture' has suffered from misconceptions and is often perceived as a 'fluffy' response to dealing with challenging children. It is regularly misunderstood and seen as being soft on children rather than providing appropriate opportunities for children to engage in the sorts of nurturing activities and experiences that they may have missed out on in early childhood. These may include simple activities such as preparing and eating meals together, learning how to work in supportive groups or playing together. Using social stories or designing self-reflection activities can help develop emotional regulation skills, as can simple activities such as cooking or craft.

When facilitated properly, these nurturing, developmental experiences allow children to listen and be listened to. They are encouraged and supported to develop their social skills with adults who model positive behaviours. Sharing is encouraged through activities that include social breakfasts and lunches. The focus is on developing self-esteem and confidence – providing an environment that allows children to feel secure. Successful nurturing environments can also improve a child's relationship with the adults at home, as they are developing connections with adults in school that will help them to become more affectionate and caring in all settings.

The aim of this approach is for the children to develop age-appropriate behaviours by filling in the gaps left by early childhood developmental deficits. As we have said, if a child arrived in school and could not read, then we would have an obligation to teach them how: that would be the obvious and instant response. If a child arrives in school and cannot behave appropriately, we should teach them how. In some circumstances this may not be seen as the obvious response, and misbehaviour may not be viewed as a developmental deficit.

Most children will experience nurturing 'rough and tumble' activities with parents or siblings. They will wrestle and tickle each other in a physical but protected and loving manner. They learn that physical contact can be fun, but that sometimes we might accidentally get – or cause – hurt, helping to build resilience. Other children

---

7   Christie Renick, Inside the Bruce Perry Show, *The Imprint* (23 May 2018). Available at: https://imprintnews.org/news-2/inside-the-bruce-perry-show/30963.

only associate physical contact with violence and aggression. This may be because a sibling often hits them or even because they have been exposed to domestic violence. At school, these children are hypervigilant and protective. They are likely to lash out at the slightest physical contact and do not have any positive associations with being touched. These are the children who seem to get into fights a lot or who react explosively to accidental physical contact – their response is defensive.

Nurture is about much more than providing a classroom where children can go to get away from the normal rigour of mainstream lessons, where they can just eat cake and drink juice. It is not a way of hiding children away and lowering their expectations and those of their teachers. It certainly is not about asking a teaching assistant to 'look after' kids and play games with them in a room full of bean bags so that they do not disrupt the real lesson.

Real nurture is based on a set of principles that form the basis of an understanding approach:

- It is important that you understand child development and understand how the brain impacts on behaviour.

- Schools, classrooms and adult relationships must be safe for all children – their well-being is crucial.

- The choice of language you use with the children will underpin the development of strong, supportive relationships.

- You must interpret the children's behaviour as a form of communication (that does not excuse poor behaviour, but it can make it easier to deal with).

- You must understand and support the transitional phases of a child's life.

If you are serious about using nurture as a genuine intervention, then basing your approach on these key principles will allow you to do it properly. You must consider neural development and how a child is influenced by their environment. You must ensure that they are educated in an emotionally safe space, that children's well-being and care is of high priority and that you learn to use language skilfully and appropriately (for more on this, see Chapter Eight). Understanding behaviour as a way in which children are seeking to communicate is vital, as is recognising the impact of transitions on children's emotions.

Transitions

Transitions can be stressful and a cause of anxiety for many children. They can develop the same feelings we associate with loss and even bereavement. If a child moves schools or classes, they might be leaving a strong protective relationship, one that helps them to feel safe and accepted. If a member of staff leaves, this too can be destabilising for a child who has formed a close connection with the adult concerned. As they move to a new environment, they might arrive with heightened anxiety and need support to work through that sense of loss.

We all feel a degree of nervousness and anxiety when we meet new people or join a new group. Imagine how this must feel for a vulnerable child who moves from a small, nurturing primary school to a secondary school with 2,000 pupils. As teachers and leaders, we need to be super vigilant in how we support the most vulnerable pupils through these transitions – we need to be aware of the potential stress felt by these children and respond to it appropriately. Schools can provide a supportive and nurturing environment in which children feel safe, understood and loved – or they can create anxiety through fear and the threat of punishment. You decide which environment you create.

Stress and anxiety – yours and theirs

Stress level: extreme. It's like she was a jar with the lid screwed on too tight, and inside the jar were pickles, angry pickles, and they were fermenting, and about to explode.

Fiona Wood[8]

Understanding stress and its impact on behaviour will further help you to emotionally adjust to the challenge you face in the classroom and across the school. Understanding your own stress helps you when it comes to your interactions with the children. When dealing with stressed children, it is vital that the adult adjusts.

---

8   Fiona Wood, *Six Impossible Things* (New York and Boston: Little, Brown and Company, 2015), p. 11.

You must remain calm and allow them to de-escalate to your level, or they will suck you into their chaos. Too often we see angry adults trying to deal with angry children, which is not helpful and just fans the flames. It is also not healthy for relationships and can heighten anxiety for both parties. Angry children may also seek revenge, and the last thing you need is a child holding a grudge against you. Working in an environment in which you regularly find yourself stressed and angry is damaging to your health and will impact on every aspect of your work, which may also put pressure on your homelife.

I can recall standing in the reception area of a large secondary school in the north of England. As I was signing in to attend a meeting, I was unable to avoid observing a 'confrontation' between a pupil and an adult male, wearing a blue suit and brown 'leadership' brogues. The six-foot-tall boy – a Year 10 or 11 pupil, at best guess – had walked through reception when that was clearly forbidden. I am guessing that it was the quickest route and that he probably took it often. The teacher stopped him, stood directly in front of him and immediately started shouting. With a mere twelve inches between their faces he was shouting and accidently spitting in a furious rage because this young man had dared to walk through an out-of-bounds area. Sweat was dripping from his temples, his face was bright red and everyone in reception had come to a standstill to observe the altercation.

After a few minutes of what can only be described as ranting, the boy just casually shrugged his shoulders, turned and walked slowly away to join his laughing mates, who were loving the show from beyond the glass doors. The pupil was wrong for walking through reception if the rules say otherwise; however, the teacher escalated that interaction, created stress and anxiety for himself and probably had very little impact on the pupil. I suspect that was not the last time the young man took that shortcut. As teachers, we need to protect ourselves from that level of stress and make sure our interactions with children are calm and assertive rather than angry and demanding.

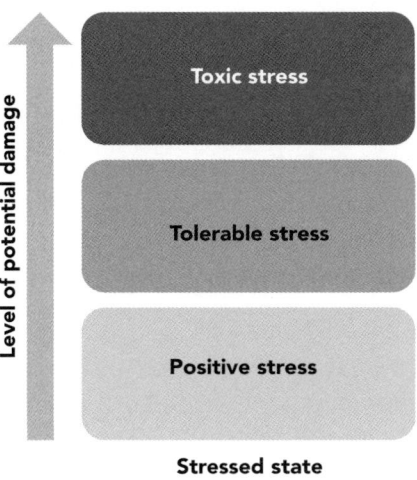

We can think of stress as manifesting at three different levels:[9]

1. **Positive stress** is the kind of stress that everyone feels easily, quickly and regularly. It is the daily pressure we often experience when doing our job or dealing with daily relational interactions. It is the sort of pressure that we can easily handle on a day-to-day basis. We need positive stress – it builds resilience and trains us in how to cope. It releases cortisol and adrenaline into our bodies in manageable amounts, priming us for action. As teachers, we provide positive stresses for pupils. We put them, consciously, in positively stressful scenarios almost every day. This might be through the pressure of coursework, a lesson activity or homework. It may be an exam or a test. Every one of these activities builds resilience – as long as the stress remains positive.

2. **Tolerable stress** is that longer lasting, more intense stress that everyone comes across in varying degrees of regularity. It is the stress you feel over a prolonged period of time when work is not going well or your personal relationships are suffering. It may be that you are struggling financially or

9   National Scientific Council on the Developing Child, *Excessive Stress Disrupts the Architecture of the Developing Brain*. Working Paper No. 3 (Cambridge, MA: Harvard University Center on the Developing Child, 2014). Available at: https://developingchild. harvard.edu/wp-content/uploads/2005/05/Stress_Disrupts_Architecture_Developing_ Brain-1.pdf.

have suffered a bereavement or loss. Tolerable stress can be managed with the help of supportive relationships: the close and reliable bonds we have with partners, friends and trusted colleagues. This may just be in the form of a drink with a friend on a Friday night or the enjoyment of being a member of a club or social group. Supportive connections come from strong relationships, established over time. The people in your life help you to deal with your stress and you, in turn, help them. Supportive relationships help keep the hormone balance in your body right by increasing your serotonin levels and decreasing the release of cortisol. Serotonin helps to stabilise your mood and give you a feeling of well-being. Without these relationships, stress can manifest and grow. Stress can have a cumulative effect and very quickly become toxic.

3. **Toxic stress** occurs when stress levels become dangerous. Toxic stress can be related to trauma, ACEs, neglect, abuse, serious loss and illness. The lack of supportive relationships will allow toxic stress to grow and not subside. The body floods with dangerous levels of cortisol, making us more susceptible to damaging conditions. Toxic stress can weaken the immune system and cause heart disease, high blood pressure and high blood sugar. It can eventually lead to anxiety and depression, nerve problems and digestive issues. Toxic stress can be controlled, or even prevented, by protective relationships, which are a level above supportive relationships. The strongest protective relationships come from parents and caregivers: those with the ability to provide unconditional positive regard, always. However, without these protective relationships, the toxic stress will continue. We know that many children are not protected by these relationships, that they have been exposed to numerous ACEs without the means of repair.

Bruce D. Perry emphasises that we should not be afraid of stress and that stress itself can, and does, lead to either resilience or vulnerability. This is dependent on what he refers to as 'patterns of stress activation' and can be seen in the following figure. This shows that stress can be good for you if it is present in the right way. The aim is to shift unpredictable, extreme and prolonged activations of stress over to predictable, moderate and controllable activations.

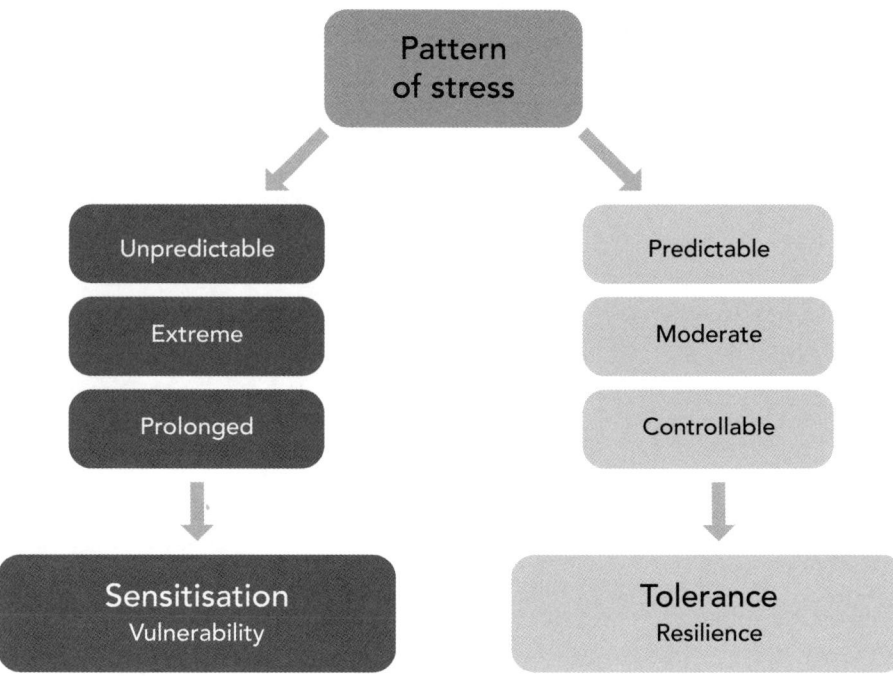

Try this

■ If you are a school leader, consider the role of key adults at your school. Provide the most vulnerable children with a trusted adult – someone who can develop a strong relationship with a pupil who may lack a protective relationship at home. Allow the trusted adult check-in time every day, with the remit of acting like a supportive caregiver. If you can, provide check-out time at the end of the day too. Check on the welfare of the child: ask whether they have managed to do their homework, ask them how they are, laugh and joke with them. Provide the child with a trusting relationship and a safe space, both physically and emotionally. The aim of the trusted adult is to provide positive and healthy relational experiences. This may take time to embed but allows the child to feel understood and grow in confidence. Your aim, as the leader, is to provide authentic care. There are great adults in schools who can perform this role: it might be that you use office, estates or catering staff. With a bit of training, they could really offer a child the relationship they need to feel supported and accepted. Your school culture should create psychological safety for the children, and having a trusted adult to turn to will help to achieve this.

- If you are a teacher, make sure you show self-restraint when dealing with agitated pupils. If you are talking to a stressed child, you will need to calm the situation first and not look for immediate compliance. Recognise when you are responding in a stressed way yourself and, if necessary, ask another adult to step in. Do not be afraid to remove yourself from the situation if you can see it is only escalating. Model appropriate responses to stress as children will follow your example: you are the role model. We will learn about de-escalation techniques in Chapter Eight, and you can use these to help you deal with pupils' stress responses.

Sometimes the smallest thing can elicit what we perceive as a totally disproportional response from a child. They might 'flip their lid' over something we barely registered or have, what appears on the surface, a ridiculous reaction to a very minor incident or event. Although the response may seem ludicrous to us, there is a very simple explanation as to why this happens: a child is unable to engage their upper brain and therefore their ability to make rational decisions disappears.

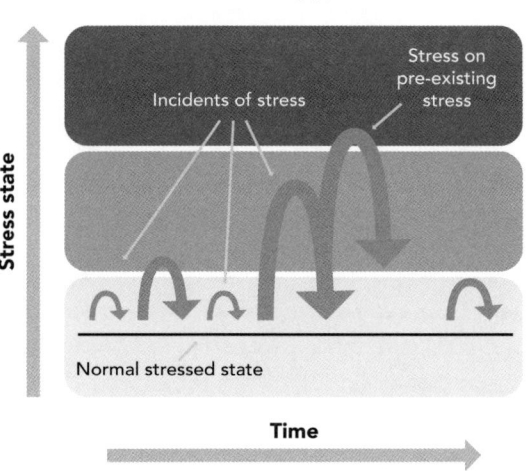

Sensitising pattern

This diagram (adapted from the work of Bruce Perry)[10] shows a normal level of stress as a flat line over time. This is where we operate on a day-to-day basis. After we experience individual stressful incidents we return to the 'normal' line as our stress subsides. These incidents usually keep us in the positive stress state. However, on some occasions we may suffer from more significant levels of stress that may take us into the next state – that of tolerable stress – but we still return to normal when the triggering incident is successfully resolved. However, the diagram indicates that sometimes we can experience a new stressful incident whilst still dealing with a previous event. This stress on pre-existing stress takes us into the danger zone of toxic stress. However, as we can see from the diagram, if we are able to deal with the stress, it recedes over time and we return to normal. This pattern repeats throughout our lifetime. We can return to normal through our exposure to supportive and protective relationships.

Supportive and protective relationships allow us to deal with stress and resolve issues; they give us resilience. When those relationships are absent, the picture can be very different.

---

10 Adapted from Bruce Perry's conference keynote slides from *What Works: Creating a Culture of Trauma Responsive Practice in Scotland*, Grand Central Hotel, Glasgow, 5 November 2019 (original slides from 2018).

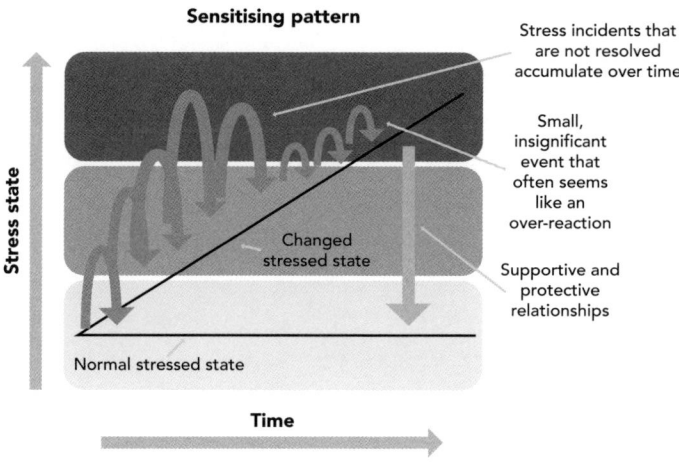

This diagram shows us how stress can be constant. The child is exposed to extreme and continuously stressful conditions. Over time, the normal stress state changes and it becomes impossible to return to the baseline level. The smallest incidents and events are now having much more impact until, as the diagram shows, the child is consistently embedded in a heightened and toxic state of stress. We can see how we might struggle to understand why a child has a (perceived) overreaction. Our challenge is to help the child return to the baseline, which can only be achieved through providing supportive and, in the most severe cases, protective relationships. If children are not feeling safe and are in a constant state of stress, they will continue to struggle to access their upper brain. They are unable to make rational decisions and will continue to make poor choices and judgements.

> Unlike simple stress, trauma changes your view of your life and yourself. It shatters your most basic assumptions about yourself and your world – 'Life is good,' 'I'm safe,' 'People are kind,' 'I can trust others,' 'The future is likely to be good' – and replaces them with feelings like 'The world is dangerous,' 'I can't win,' 'I can't trust other people,' or 'There's no hope.'
>
> **Mark Goulston**[11]

---

11 Mark Goulston, *Post-Traumatic Stress Disorder for Dummies* (Hoboken, NJ: Wiley, 2008), p. 23.

Chapter Eight

Conflict resolution, de-escalation and the power of language

Revenge and retaliation always perpetuate the cycle of anger, fear and violence.

Coretta Scott King[1]

The behaviour is just a symptom

When dealing with conflict it is important to remember that we are tackling the primitive brain and the fight-or-flight, or freeze, response. It is crucial to understand how feelings and emotions may be driving behaviours, and that by reacting only to the behaviour, conflict may be increased. Experiences and memories drive emotions and feelings – this then creates our behaviour responses. Behaviour then creates experiences and memories, which leads to the cycle beginning again.

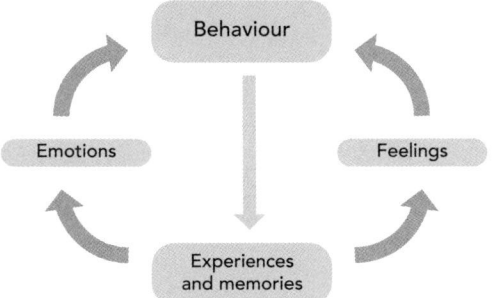

---

1   Janet Kinosian, Q&A with the Late Coretta Scott King, *Huffington Post* [blog] (23 June 2009). Available at: https://www.huffpost.com/entry/qa-with-the-late-coretta_b_94899.

It is natural for us, as teachers, to concentrate on dealing with just the behaviour without considering our pupils' emotions and feelings. However, this is equivalent to a doctor dealing with just the symptoms of an illness, rather than looking for a cure or cause. Our responsibility is to help children deal with conflict by understanding the experiences that may be causing their emotions and feelings, and thus their behaviour. Once we understand the cause of the behaviour it becomes easier to change. But as we know, before we change behaviour we may have to de-escalate and mange short-term conflict.

If a child throws a chair across the classroom, it is natural for a teacher to respond immediately to this behaviour. The response is likely to be a reprimand, removal from the class or a sanction. In this case, the teacher is not considering the feelings or emotions that have triggered the behaviour; they are dealing with the behaviour alone. If a teacher throws a chair across the staffroom, would the response be the same? I would suggest that if you witnessed another adult throwing a chair then you would immediately offer concerned support. You would worry about their emotional state and offer help, wondering why they had reacted by throwing a chair, and assuming that something awful must have triggered this outburst. You would not shout at them or reprimand them; you would probably want to give them a supportive hug. In both cases the behaviour has been driven by feelings, yet our responses are different. The adult gets empathy and support; the child gets criticism and punishment.

Understanding the causes of conflict (what might be driving emotions and feelings) will therefore help us to deal with it in a relational way. Causes can be broken down into several categories:

- **Revenge:** Children will often seek revenge if they feel that they have suffered an injustice. In some cases, children will recruit their friends to help them deliver revenge and this can lead to extreme conflict if not managed or foreseen. We call this a flock response.

- **Communication breakdown:** There may be a frustrating lack of clarity from the adults about expectations, routines and rules. This may also be prompted by a task or an activity that is not clearly explained or appropriately differentiated.

- **Trauma:** There may be conflict associated with a child's window of tolerance and their inability to regulate during certain activities or during particular interactions. Sometimes children are exposed to memories and experiences that trigger emotional responses. In the most extreme circumstances, this conflict can be severe or even dangerous, and escalate quickly.

- **Anxiety:** A stressful situation might cause conflict due to a child's already anxious state; however, to others the situation might not necessarily seem stressful and they will struggle to pre-empt or understand the response. Again, the cause might be an emotional response to a memory or experience. The reaction can happen quickly, without warning, and be extreme.

- **Power-seeking or attention-needing:** The term attention-seeking is often used when describing children's behaviour in class. If you view this slightly differently, as 'attention-needing', then it will help to frame your response. A child may 'need' attention but seek it in an inappropriate way. If you provide them with the attention they need, in an appropriate way, then they will not continue to demand it inappropriately. The brain seeks what it needs and will do so through whatever means it can.

- **Not getting the balance of challenge and support right:** As discussed earlier when we looked at the social discipline window, too much challenge without support, or too much support without challenge, can cause conflict.

The power of the restorative conversation

I clearly remember an incident with an extremely troubled Year 11 pupil – Michael – who was in crisis during a PE lesson. Michael had lashed out in frustration and accidently caught a teaching assistant with his flailing arm. The teaching assistant was shocked and hurt – it was one of those horrible situations in which he was genuinely and compassionately trying to help Michael but began to get angry because Michael was not responding to his increasingly agitated requests. He ended up getting too close and the boy lashed out. On this occasion the experienced member of staff, under pressure, had not thought through the process of regulation. He had not, as discussed previously, used regulation as the first phase of dealing with a child in crisis; co-regulation had not taken place and the situation had escalated. An angry adult was trying to deal with an angry boy.

Later, Michael and I met in my office to discuss the incident. He sat, head in hands, crying. His remorse was real, and together we were able to articulate how he had made the teaching assistant feel. I simply asked Michael to explain, from his point of view, what had happened and how it had made him feel. He was able to reflect and to consider his feelings during and after the incident. I then asked him how he thought others around him had been affected, and it was clear that he was aware of his impact on the teaching assistant. He then sobbed as he told me about 'stuff' that was happening at home. He had arrived at school angry and upset that morning, having literally just had a physical fight with his stepfather. His home life was difficult: his dad was in prison, his mum was in a violent relationship and he spent most of his time at home fighting and arguing with his mum's partner.

Michael liked this member of staff; they had a strong relationship and he was truly upset that he had jeopardised it. He wanted to make things right, repair the damage and move on. I was proud of how he had reflected and was showing empathy and a desire to repair the damage. I took him to see the teaching assistant, who had also reflected, and they sat and talked through the incident. It was genuinely moving to see the repair and reparation happening in front of my eyes. There was authentic care in action – on both sides. The member of staff was happy that they were able to discuss the incident and move on. He felt that his relationship with Michael was now stronger than it had been and that he too had learnt about his own reactions and how they can impact on Michael's responses.

However, it was not long after the young man had returned to class – still a bit upset and quiet – that I received a request to see his class teacher. The teacher wanted him removed from class and even suggested that he needed to be excluded. Despite all that had happened that day, Michael was settled in class, subdued and quietly getting on with his work. The teacher simply wanted a sanction – revenge for the incident and for Michael to be punished for his actions. This was a shock to me and an attitude that was very rarely seen in the school. I saw this as an opportunity to reset the teacher's values, and to create a chance for him to reflect on his attitude and his role as a trusted adult. So, the process started again, only this time adult to adult.

I asked him to reflect, to think about his feelings and Michael's. I asked him why he felt that a punishment was appropriate and what impact he thought excluding Michael would have. I asked him to consider what would happen to his ongoing relationship with Michael if he were to be excluded for a few days and then returned into his class. It took about one minute of calm conversation before I could see the teacher's whole physical bearing change. He began to apologise for his response and was ashamed that he had demanded a sanction. This was both a lovely and powerful conversation. He was – at heart – a great, caring and compassionate teacher who had simply lapsed from a position he truly believed in. A relational approach and the simple power of restorative language and reflection had worked. At no time was blame used as a tool to extract a specific response. The reflections, with Michael and with both adults, had been honest and fair. All three of them finished with their pride intact, relationships stronger and values of which they could be proud.

Perhaps you feel that this was a soft response, or know that it would be considered as such in your school? You may feel that a sanction should – nay, must – be administered following an incident of this nature. All I argue is that using this approach, along with restorative language and a willingness to empathise, will have a far longer lasting impact on everyone involved. Together we resolved a problem, moved on and created the opportunity for trust and safety to remain intact.

Try this

▨ If you are a head teacher or principal, consider introducing some specific staff development on the use of restorative practice. Invest in training so that staff are confident in its use and believe in the approach. It is important not to be half-hearted. Any training needs to be thorough and delivered by experts.

▨ If you are an adult in a school, whose job involves dealing with conflict resolution, use a simple restorative approach when dealing with an incident. Use the following questions, calmly and confidently:

▽ Can you tell me what happened? (The child begins to reflect.)

▽ Who was affected by what happened? (The child begins to empathise.)

▼ What can *we* do to put things right? (The child takes responsibility but knows you are there to support the process.)

▪ If you are feeling more confident and would like to develop more connections, then try the following sequence of questions:

▼ Can you tell me what happened?

▼ What were you thinking at the time?

▼ What are you thinking about now?

▼ How did it make you feel?

▼ Who else has been affected by what happened?

▼ What has been the hardest thing for you?

▼ What do we need to do to put things right?

This is a very simple introduction to the use of restorative conversation, but worth trying and practising, nonetheless. I have used this approach many, many times with success and without the need to resort to a behaviourist position. Whilst some might say that this is a soft approach, I do not see it at all, and believe it is far harder for a child to genuinely express themselves than it is for them to take an imposed sanction. The child will feel empowered and their relationships will remain intact if this approach is used. Restorative approaches can be woven into the culture of the school but only if the adults embrace and believe in them. Restorative practice, like many other approaches to managing behaviour, will not work if you do not believe in it. Authenticity is vital to successful restorative conversations, and it won't work if you don't believe that it has impact. Again, restorative practice can polarise views and you will see it being discredited. There are many champions[2] out there and many who look to condemn it. My simple advice is to not only try it but commit to it.

---

2   Try reading Mark Finnis, *Independent Thinking on Restorative Practice: Building Relationships, Improving Behaviour and Creating Stronger Communities* (Carmarthen: Independent Thinking Press, 2021).

Language matters

When considering the use of language and the importance of its skilful application in helping to manage behaviour, then the work of Bill Rogers is a great starting point.[3] Rogers helps us understand the importance of cleverly constructing sentences so that a teacher can remain assertive. We can look at language in three broad categories to help us understand how to use appropriate communication – both spoken and body language. First, we must avoid demand language. This means that we fail to regulate ourselves and so our interaction is angry, out-of-control, shouty and potentially aggressive. We might forget ourselves and adopt an aggressive stance, follow pupils or get too close to them. Some adults might purposely shout in order to scare or intimidate and gain compliance through fear.

Second, and also something to avoid, is cajoling language, which is essentially try-ing to gain compliance when we lack control and are begging children to follow our instructions. This can often be a problem when schools are attempting to follow a relational approach: staff might need constant reminders not to cajole children and that being kind does not mean pleading for their compliance. On numerous occasions I have witnessed staff, with very good intentions, cajoling children, but in doing so they lose control and the children can see that they have gained it. This is unhelpful, and although done with good intentions, can escalate problems and develop unwanted traits in the children's behaviour. They will learn that certain staff can be manipulated and that they themselves can take charge of the situation.

Therefore, the focus must be on the use of assertive language. Adults can be in con-trol of a situation, with clearly established expectations and high standards, without resorting to shouting, humiliation or aggression as a tool for compliance. Never engage in a power struggle with a pupil; it is better to walk away with the guarantee that you will discuss things later than to fall into a win-lose verbal exchange with a child. We must avoid retaliation and provide the opportunity for the child to take responsibility. When being assertive, it is important to avoid negotiation (cajoling), and instead outline firm boundaries and expectations. Choices can be given, but they must be on the adults' terms and there can't be one obvious cop-out option.

---

3   Bill Rogers, *Classroom Behaviour: A Practical Guide to Effective Teaching, Behaviour Management and Colleague Support*, 4th edn (London: SAGE Publications, 2015).

Unless the children have solid expectations in place then they will continue to push boundaries.

Adults need to catch children being good and praise them within earshot of those who may not be complying. This is sometimes known as 'tactical ignoring' and means that the child who may need attention does not get it by behaving inappropriately. In this case, we openly praise good behaviour and 'ignore' unwanted behaviour. Children will then see that they get the adult's attention when they are following instructions and behaving well.

Applying simple rule reminders is important, and saying 'thank you', rather than 'please', can be a powerful way to get children to recognise that you expect them to follow the rules; you are not asking them to. Non-verbal gestures can be used, like a simple thumbs-up or a smile, to praise children for following instructions. Remember, verbal praise should be specific rather than a general 'well done'. You can build a personalised connection through praise by simply saying 'I like it when you ...' or 'I really like how you have done ...'

Simple but clever language shifts will give you a head start when managing behaviour. Using the language of choice will allow you to give the children options that you control. This can work well with children who struggle with accepting direction and the demands of adults. Offering a limited choice will give the child the perception of control, but you are ultimately making the decision. For example, 'There are five minutes left of the lesson. You can choose to complete your work in five minutes' time or now.' This is more effective than telling a child: 'If you don't finish your work now, you will have to do it at break time.' If you offer a choice, then only give two options and give your preferred one last. Similarly, rather than reprimanding a child for doing something they should not be – 'Stop doing that!' – try asking 'What should you be doing?' Asking this question means that they will need to consider an answer, engaging their upstairs brain and making a connection.

It is also important to be positive yet assertive, rather than negative, in your instructions and interactions. This can be achieved by saying something as simple as 'I need you to walk in the corridor, thank you' rather than 'please stop running'. Tell the child what you want them to do, rather than what you do not want them to do. In this example, you are also thanking them before they have done it, indicating that you expect their cooperation. These are just some examples of how simple but clever alterations of language can be highly effective when dealing with challenging behaviour. In Chapter Six we mentioned the use of curiosity in our language and we can also take advantage of simple therapeutic language.

This is something that we introduced at my school with the help of, and training by, psychotherapists. We felt that their specialist language techniques would be powerful for all adults to use when dealing with conflict and challenging behaviour. These are simple but effective and include things like the use of silence – giving children the opportunity to talk without interruption. This will allow them time and confidence to talk about topics that they may otherwise not broach. It can be difficult to allow silence and it takes confidence and a conscious effort not to fill gaps in a conversation. It is also important to be accepting of whatever the child says. Acceptance does not mean that you agree, but it lets the child know that you understand them. You can then open up a conversation by asking a broad question – such as 'What would you like to talk about?' and then 'Can you explain that to me?' – and seeking clarification.

It is important to recognise the power of listening. In school we refer to this as 'active listening', again taken from the work of psychotherapists. During active listening the adult will simply nod and offer non-verbal cues so that children are encouraged to carry on talking. You are automatically buying into them and showing a commitment to listening. You may respond briefly by saying things like 'I see' or 'What happened then?'

This therapeutic style links very neatly with restorative conversation, during which the child is asked to explain what happened – and what they were thinking and feeling – and the adult simply guides and facilitates. The child reflects, empathises and sequences the event or incident. You, as the facilitator, can offer a summary and confirm with the child that what you have summarised is correct. These conversations allow you to grow relationships and build trust. You are relating to the child, and when you have established trust you can challenge them and look to repair any harm or damage that has occurred – either physical or emotional.

In Chapter Six we discussed the three-step process of regulate, relate, repair as a framework for responding to an incident or, in this case, resolving conflict. Language is a powerful element in this sequence and, as in many cases of conflict resolution, de-escalation and deflection is needed to allow regulation to take place. The aim of de-escalation is to slow down an incident, not to gain immediate compliance. The focus is on reducing stress levels and preventing further crisis.

Your own calm response will allow de-escalation to happen and, as mentioned earlier, you must invite the child to join you in your calm rather you joining them in their chaos. It is OK to step away and permit a colleague to take over. This can be an instant de-escalation technique, especially if you have been directly involved in the initial conflict yourself. You must not feel that stepping away is some sort of defeat. I have often heard adults say, 'but that means that they have won' when they have been asked to walk away or if they are not able to deliver a sanction. We need to remember that we are not at war with the children and we must take the mature and controlled route that they may not be capable of navigating at that time. If the incident is dealt with correctly, the repair phase will follow later, therefore nobody has 'won'.

Try this

If you are an adult in a school, then try these simple deflection and distraction techniques when dealing with conflict resolution (you might be surprised at the reaction you get):

- Wear odd socks – the funnier the better. You will be amazed at how quickly a child will forget the incident they are involved in when they see your socks. They will want to know why you have odd socks on, so have a story ready.

- Learn a magic trick. This sparks children's curiosity and thus allows them to engage their upstairs brain – allowing them to regulate.

- Gain knowledge of the child's likes. A member of staff at my school once learnt the names of 150 Pokémon characters to help him connect with one child.[4] You can use their interests to strike up a conversation or ask a question to begin forming a connection.

---

4   This child was considered spoilt by some of his peers, and even by some staff, because of all the cards that his parents had bought for him. However, they were a substitute for giving him attention, love, clean clothes and a clean house. They were a way of keeping him occupied so they did not need to. He needed authentic care and connection, which he got at school.

- Ask a simple question such as 'Where do you live?' This is a great starter for a deflection conversation as everyone has an answer. The challenge for you is to be able to expand that conversation by responding with questions about the local area, the park, the estate, or anything else you can think of. Within minutes you will be chatting away calmly and talking about them – you will have made a connection.

- Point something out that you can ask a question or tell a story about. This works best if it is something unusual, perhaps outside a window or in the sky. Cloud shapes can be interesting to look at and can stimulate conversation. This, again, is using children's curiosity to reduce stress and deflect attention from the incident.

- Offer the child a crunchy or chewy snack and encourage them to bite with their back teeth for calming (or, to up-regulate, suck a peppermint sweet).

- Use a gym ball. Get the child to lay on their tummy and apply pressure across their back with a gym ball to help them to calm.

- Use a TheraBand (one of those stretchy bands you get from a physiotherapist). Ask a child to hold one with both hands and see how far they can pull it. Or start doing it yourself and their curiosity will take over and they will want a go. There are lots of things you can do with these bands that quickly deliver deep pressure and aid regulation. If you stretch the band between the two front legs of a child's chair, they can push their legs against it whilst sitting in class. This gives them the deep pressure they need whilst they sit in the lesson doing their work.

- Use hand cream to give a simple hand massage – make a game out of it such as thumb war. Again, the pressure can help with mood regulation.

- Carry something unusual in your pocket. This will allow you to ask a simple deflection question such as, 'I've found something but I'm not sure what it is. I wonder if you could help me?' The child will be curious and immediately distracted.

Distraction, not reaction

Once, on a school trip to the coast, one of the children ran away across the beach and was attempting to climb a sheer cliff face. This was an extreme situation with a potentially very dangerous outcome. If not handled correctly, the child could have got into a very precarious position and the consequences could have been serious. Luke, our care team leader (some schools would use the term 'behaviour support workers' but we choose to use the term 'care'), followed him at a safe distance, knowing that if he was to shout at or chase him, he would have gone further up the cliff, in an attempt to get further away from the adults. The boy looked clearly distressed and highly anxious. At this point Luke reached into his pocket and pulled out some strange, metal, magnetic beans that he kept for moments such as these. He began to throw them up into the air and as they banged together, they made an unusual sound. The boy immediately looked at Luke with curiosity in his eyes – instantly distracted from his attempt to scale the rocky cliff.

Luke simply asked, 'Do you know why they make that noise?' Immediately stopping his ascent, the pupil quickly replied, 'What even are they?' This was the small window Luke needed in order to establish a connection, so he was able to approach the child and sit down on a rock next to him. 'Have a go,' he said, and he threw the strange beans towards the boy. He began to throw and catch them with a smile on his face. They were then able to discuss why he ran off to the cliff and the process of repair was set in motion before heading back to the bus. This was the work of a skilled adult who had seen an incident happening and responded calmly and with expertise. He was also thoroughly prepared, with his crazy magnetic beans in his pocket.

Model communication

When talking to children, we should obviously think about our own manners. Are we being polite? Are we being kind? How do we like to be talked to by others? What do we believe to be an appropriate way of talking to others? Something as simple as saying sorry to a child is powerful when developing relationships. Some adults will feel that apologising to children is a sign of weakness, even if they have made a mistake or got something wrong. I would suggest that it shows confidence and maturity. It means that you are willing to accept responsibility in the same way that you would expect a child to. You are modelling responsible behaviour; therefore, a simple 'sorry' will have a huge impact on future relationships.

Remember to be curious and empathetic. You can show this by saying something as simple as, 'I wonder if this is happening because something has upset you?' By telling the child that you understand that they may be upset, you are showing empathy and attuning to them – you are making that connection. This allows us to deal with and correct behaviour without damaging relationships.

Revise your view of conflict

Staff mindset and perceptions play a role in dealing with conflict and this can be influenced by language. If a child is behaving in a challenging way and there is conflict, then the pre-existing mindset of the staff will impact on the way in which they respond to that incident. If we expect to see a naughty child, then that is what we will see. If we expect to see a child in need of support, then that is what we will see. In my school we adopted a protocol for communicating with staff during an incident. We stopped reporting that a child was 'kicking off' or 'out of control'. We stopped referring to children 'causing problems' and began to talk in terms of children 'needing support'. This means that staff attending incidents now do so with the intention of offering support to a child. The culture and mindset is one of support, and this was made possible by simple changes in phrasing. This, again, may be perceived by some as a soft approach, but it worked to alter our starting point for incident management. A child in crisis needs support and we are there to offer that support.

Consider yourself a translator; you are seeing behaviour and translating it into communication. Yes, you must deal with conflict immediately to prevent any harm being done to anyone involved and, yes, you have a professional responsibility to keep children safe. However, you can also learn from conflicts and incidents once they are over. Post-incident learning is time spent analysing and reflecting. In this phase of conflict resolution, it is important to plan and prepare for further incidents and to mitigate future problems where possible. This is often neglected in our busy schedules, so we end up lurching from one conflict to another without learning the triggers and exploring the associated feelings and emotions. Post-incident learning can help us plan for future challenges and can even be used to help with lesson planning. It can also encourage us to involve other colleagues and professionals, looking together for an unmet need or a potential intervention. Post-incident learning can involve other colleagues and follow-up restorative conversations with the child in question. This is all part of the repair step. It is also important to remember that you cannot solve every problem.

Try this

Thirty top tips for conflict resolution and de-escalation:[5]

1. Give the illusion of choice. For example, if a child is angry, give them two options of where to go – making them feel that they are in control.

2. Offer clear structures, routines and boundaries (with high expectations).

3. Offer instant praise or reward for desired behaviours – for example, stickers, counters, verbal praise or non-verbal positive gestures.

4. Inform the children of the desired behaviour – clearly.

5. Use appropriate humour – never sarcasm.

6. Talk low, slow and quietly.

7. Offer reassurance – including positive physical prompts.

8. Divert and distract by introducing another activity or topic.

9. Set clear enforceable limits.

10. Offer alternatives, choices and options.

11. Give a child a way to 'get out' of the situation with dignity.

---

5   These are strategies developed over time by the care team (behaviour leaders) at Springwell Learning Community in Barnsley and used for training staff in SEMH, AP and mainstream settings.

12. Do not be afraid to step back and let a colleague take over.

13. Offer the use of a calm space – for example, a comfy sofa or a quiet room.

14. Be prepared to listen.

15. Know when the situation is in stalemate. Do not create a win-lose situation.

16. Be flexible in thought and response.

17. Wherever possible, show trust and allow pupils to resolve their own problems.

18. Try to look at an individual when you are making an important point; intermittent eye contact is very powerful.

19. Be aware of the signals given out by your body position and posture.

20. If you can, try to sit down when talking – or at least get on the other person's level.

21. Nod your head to indicate attentiveness.

22. Smile if appropriate – particularly to show agreement.

23. Be aware of the physical distance between yourself and the child.

24. Use hand, shoulder and whole-body gestures to support discussion.

25. Use appropriate physical contact as reassurance.

26. Acknowledge the existence of a problem.

27. Give reassurance and offer support.

28. Be aware of voice quality, pitch and power whilst making good use of pauses.

29. Paraphrase what has been said and check that it is accurate.

30. Use the word 'we' in discussion so that the solution is seen as being found together.

Sometimes we get things wrong and that is OK. However, it is also important that we have insight into what we should not do or say. Often, we may find ourselves doing or saying things without realising the consequences. Conflict can be escalated quickly if our response is not right.

Try this

Thirty top tips for things to avoid:

Do not …

1. Ever place the young person in a position of no escape.

2. Use destructive criticism, sarcasm, or belittling methods to humiliate.

3. Remind the child of previous incidents.

4. Divulge personal information in front of a group.

5. Make unrealistic threats.

6. Make insensitive or ridiculing remarks.

7. Lose your temper.

8. Make 'you will' statements.

9. Allow 'You can't make me – I won't' types of situations to develop.

10. Get involved in arguments.

11. Disagree with the other adults present.

12. Be fooled into thinking that you should be able to deal with any situation.

13. Expect colleagues to get on with it without your support.

14. Be unfair or hostile.

15. Use excessive punishments or sanctions. A sanction must be reasonable, proportionate and necessary.

16. Inflate the situation out of proportion.

17. Allow yourself to be wound up.

18. Carry on arguing if you know that you are wrong.

19. Restart the argument once calm has been achieved.

20. Use unnecessary peer group pressure.

21. Refer to family members, especially to make comparisons with siblings.

22. Invade personal space.

23. Use staring, threatening eye contact.

24. Stand over pupils in a threatening manner.

25. Appear to lack confidence.

26. Appear tense.

27. Retaliate with physical gestures.

28. Use inappropriate physical contact with a child.

29. Be oblivious to signals within the environment.

30. Appear intimidated.

Dealing with conflict is one of the hardest and most stressful parts of a teacher's role. You will get it wrong, but you'll dust yourself down and keep going – it is OK not to get it right the first time. We worry, even lose sleep, about the possibility of making mistakes and feel the weight of scrutiny from leaders and peers. But being good at behaviour management takes time and practice. So, give it time and practise the techniques you have learnt. Always remember, solving conflict is not easy – it just gets easier.

Chapter Nine

Exclusions – how do we ever justify giving up on a child?

You see, in this world there's two kinds of people, my friend. Those with loaded guns and those who dig.

Clint Eastwood[1]

This is not a radical call for the abolition of exclusions; it is simply an opportunity to reflect on the process and concept of exclusions and to ask ourselves whether they are really necessary. If, as a species, we can create nuclear fusion, send probes to the far reaches of the galaxy and find medicines to cure serious diseases, then surely we are creative enough to find a way to stop kicking kids out of school? This is not about knowingly exposing teachers to violence and abuse, or excusing challenging and dangerous behaviour, but it is about reflecting on whether exclusions work and how we can ever justify giving up on a child and their future. Teachers have a right to be safe and free from psychological and physical harm, but children also have a right to an education and to be protected from a life of underachievement and social exclusion. Yes, some children need specialist, high-cost support and intervention that is often not available in mainstream schools, and they should be able to access this. This is therefore about culture: a determination to find solutions and break free from the easy option of passing a problem to someone else via a permanent exclusion. It is about a whole profession accepting that exclusions damage the most vulnerable in society, cause lasting harm and inflict significant social and economic damage on young people. This really is about changing hearts and minds and embracing change – even if that does not happen overnight.

---

1   In character as Blondie in *The Good, the Bad and the Ugly*, dir. Sergio Leone (1966). Nothing to do with education, but it's important to understand the power of playing the long game when dealing with complex behaviours.

No-exclusions policy?

During my time in mainstream secondary education I was lucky enough to lead the inclusion department in a large urban comprehensive school. This fantastic school had 1,600 pupils on roll, from some extremely disadvantaged areas with localised economic deprivation and its associated challenges. The culture of the school was one of compassion and understanding but with an expectation of respect and aspiration. Fixed-term exclusions were high, and this was initially seen as the school taking a strong stance against challenging behaviour. It was a way of showing staff that the school and its leaders did not tolerate children who were abusive and defiant and that the systems would support staff by using exclusion as a clear and consistent sanction (there it is again – consistency).

However, it quickly became clear that the exclusion rate was remaining high – too high. Children were being excluded repeatedly and not changing their behaviour as a consequence. The culture was quickly becoming confrontational: incident followed by punishment, then resentment and relational damage. Pupils would swear at staff, be excluded, have a day off playing Mega Drive,[2] then return to school and swear at staff again. This was the cycle that we were in – trapped by a behaviour policy that used exclusion in the naive hope that children would stop swearing and be 'cured' of their behaviour problems. We were lucky, though, because we had a head teacher who was willing and able to change. He knew that the system was failing and encouraged creative and innovative responses. He was also willing to commit resources and training to finding a solution, knowing that the school needed a culture- and values-driven response to an escalating problem.

For the next three years, the school did not issue a single fixed-term exclusion. Instead, we developed a system of restorative practice, thoughtful and positive separation from the mainstream and then supported reintegration. We used isolation that was not really isolation. There were no booths; children were taught in small classes for short periods of time away from their peers. The focus was on restoration and repair, not on punishment. The staff were well-trained relational specialists and cared deeply about the children. The leadership team believed in the approach

---

2   This is a games console from the days before PlayStation and Xbox – for those of us old enough to remember. This will give you a hint at the time period I am discussing here.

and backed it – and with some of them it was a difficult task to get them to embrace it initially.

We did not tolerate abuse to teachers or disruptive behaviour – we just took exclusion away as an option and backed ourselves to be creative enough to find other ones. The school did not fall into chaos: children developed greater respect for adults, incidents of abuse and swearing reduced dramatically and a positive culture was restored. We used a relational model to eradicate the use of exclusions. During that time there were no permanent exclusions and pupils requiring additional help with managing their behaviour were taken through a supportive assessment process, and, where appropriate, an alternative option – such as vocational learning and outdoor education – was used. This was achieved by developing our own alternative curriculum pathways so we didn't have to rely on an external offer. This was an example of a school taking responsibility for all its pupils and, to coin an old term, every child mattered. The thing about this head teacher was that he was not refusing to use exclusions at that point; he would have used exclusions if they were necessary. But they were just not needed. The school did not have a no-exclusions policy; it just had a commitment to trying to do the right thing. We shifted the default response away from exclusion.

What does the exclusion rate say about a school?

So, why is there so much controversy and divided opinion about the use of exclusions? As with many behaviour-related issues, the exclusion debate rolls on and on. It divides the views of highly experienced and well-regarded professionals at all levels and ignites the interest of the media and the public. Let's face it, if you want to improve a school's performance quickly, then excluding a load of the worst-behaved kids will help massively. If a school is judged on how quickly it improves, then exclusions will always be a tool for fast-track improvement. Therefore, as a school leader, who is judged on school improvement (and at risk of losing your job), you will always be tempted to exclude those children who do not immediately conform. However, if schools were judged on how infrequently they exclude children, and inclusion was a prerequisite for excellence, then schools simply would not exclude. They would invest time, effort and resources into finding creative solutions to reducing exclusions.

Is a school great because it uses exclusions? Does this show a strong stance and a commitment to culture change? Or is a school great because it does not use exclusions? The major problem with the exclusion debate is the misconceptions and assumptions associated with reducing exclusions. Many believe that a reduction in exclusions means a decline in standards and an acceptance that teachers and pupils will be exposed to violence and continuous low-level disruption. This is simply not the case. There is not a trade-off between exclusions and standards. Reducing exclusions, like relational behaviour management, is not about letting kids 'get away with it'. It is still possible to reduce, and even eradicate, exclusions whilst maintaining high standards and not compromising the safety of staff and pupils. These conditions must be attached to any reduction in exclusions. If we can get this misunderstanding out of our minds, we can begin to think about genuine and committed ways to do things differently.

Another popular misconception is that schools that have reduced their exclusion rates must somehow be cheating the system. Cynically, the line of thought goes that if a school does not use permanent exclusions, surely it must be getting rid of kids through other, less ethical means – often referred to as 'off-rolling' or 'legally' moving children to other settings within their own system. The assumption is made because this obviously does happen in some schools, but it does not mean that this is the only way to reduce exclusions. This is something that I have been accused of myself when publicly celebrating zero permanent exclusions. I was accused of 'moving' children to other schools to hide exclusions – and that just simply has not happened.

As we have seen throughout this book, the adoption of relational behaviour practice takes time, dedication and resources. It needs determination from leaders and enthusiasm from all adults to make it work. We also need Ofsted to look carefully at how they judge schools, and link that to inclusion: schools should not be outstanding if they rely heavily on fixed-term exclusions. Some schools, held in high regard by 'the system', have children losing up to 40 days a year through fixed-term exclusion. How can that ever be justified? If a child is accumulating that many exclusions, then surely the school should be looking at support and intervention? Maybe the child needs a formal needs assessment, with a view to getting them the right support. It could be argued that high levels of exclusion show not only a lack of integrity but also an inadequate system for supporting pupils' additional needs.

The reality of fixed-term exclusion

Many children who receive fixed-term exclusions are essentially getting a day off (or numerous days off). They are at home playing video games or out wandering the streets. If we changed the name of the sanction from 'fixed-term exclusion' to 'day off', do you think as many people would support it?

'Reece will be having *two days off* to play his Xbox following the incident in maths when he told the teacher to fuck off. I have been assured that, during *these days off*, he will be spending all day playing an inappropriate game that has an 18 rating.'

'Having thrown her chips across the dinner hall, Claire will now be having *a day off* to go shopping with her mum as she needs some new trainers. She will then wear these trainers on her return to school and therefore be forced to spend the *day in isolation* for breaking uniform rules. As we already know, Claire does not respond well to being placed in the isolation booths so we will probably be giving her *two more days off* as a result of her refusal to cooperate and follow the prescribed sanction. On her return from her *extra days off*, she will still have to complete the isolation period as we believe in a consistent approach.'

If you feel that a fixed-term exclusion is necessary, then think about what is being achieved and whether it is actually going to have any impact. With some pupils it might, but with others it will have no impact at all. If an intervention has very little impact, why would we still use it?

Justified exclusions?

So, when is an exclusion justified? Is it ever justified? Although I have never permanently excluded a child, I have used fixed-term exclusions. These have always been the last resort and never framed as a punishment. They are one element in a process to develop appropriate provision and intervention. Limited fixed-term exclusions can provide breathing space and allow time for planning an intervention. They can be employed as a reset following an incident and should be used in collaboration with restorative processes or adapted provision – incorporating both support and challenge (the social discipline window, again). If they can be avoided, then they should be.

Permanent exclusion should only ever happen following a serious one-off incident. Even then, the incident must be so serious that the school leaders feel they have absolutely no other option – usually in order to protect both staff and other pupils. So, permanently excluding a child for setting off the fire alarm should never be justified – even if the behaviour policy says that's an appropriate sanction. Permanent exclusion is life-changing and therefore the school, and the head teacher, has a duty to consider the consequences and repercussions of that decision. Taking action to permanently exclude a child should be the most difficult and measured decision a head teacher and their governing body makes.

The 1966 spaghetti western *The Good, the Bad and the Ugly* can help us to think about exclusions and whether we really can justify the ultimate sanction:

- **The Good:** When things are going well, we have the best job in the world. Children behave, they progress, and we watch them grow, knowing that they will have the best care, be supported in their schooling and move successfully to their next phase of education or life. We never even consider exclusion.

- **The Bad:** Things go wrong, but we work through it. We consider the needs of the child and the contributing factors, and make the adjustments we need to support progress. We do not tolerate or excuse their challenging behaviour, but we have systems in place to help put things right. We work to make things good again. Even with sophisticated consideration, that could mean using a fixed-term exclusion to reset and buy us time. In this point, we may also consider using AP or completing a formal needs assessment for additional support. The aim is always to make things good again – we do not give up.

- **The Ugly:** There is no chance of reparation. We wash our hands of the child and the only option is to get rid of them. They become someone else's problem; we cannot see a way back.

The easy option is to give up – the ugly approach. The more difficult approach is making a commitment to putting things right and, when they go bad, trying our hardest to make them good again.

The long-term legacy of permanent exclusion

Education should be the means to break the link between demographics and destiny. Yet, every day vulnerable children are permanently excluded from our schools. These exclusions have disastrous personal and societal consequences. Many of these excluded pupils will end up in AP and contribute to worrying statistics for that cohort. The children in AP or PRUs are the country's most disadvantaged, who are four times more likely to have grown up in poverty;[3] six times more likely to have special needs;[4] ten times more likely to have mental health problems;[5] and twenty times more likely to be interacting with social services due to safeguarding concerns.[6] These children are less likely to attend other educational settings and are at risk of being involved in crime – including knife crime.[7]

Although these children may have disappeared from mainstream school, they have not disappeared from society. Their life chances are often bleak, with less than 2% of them finishing school with GCSE English and maths at grade 5 or above – and less than 5% with grade 4 or above – the qualifications they need in order to make the next step into further education or employment.[8] These children go on to make

3   As indicated by free school meal eligibility figures. See Department for Education, Permanent and Fixed-Period Exclusions in England: 2016 to 2017 [national statistics] (19 July 2018), p. 6. Available at: https://assets.publishing.service.gov.uk/government/uploads/ system/uploads/attachment_data/file/726741/text_exc1617.pdf.

4   Department for Education, Permanent and Fixed-Period Exclusions in England, p. 6.

5   Kiran Gill, with Harry Quilter-Pinner and Danny Swift, Making the Difference: Breaking the Link between School Exclusion and Social Exclusion (London: Institute for Public Policy Research, 2017), p. 7. Available at: https://www.ippr.org/files/2017-10/making-the-difference-report-october-2017.pdf.

6   Analysis from data in Department for Education, Children in Need of Help and Protection: Data and Analysis. Ref: DFE-00078-2018 (March 2018), p. 46. Available at: https://assets. publishing.service.gov.uk/government/uploads/system/uploads/attachment_data/ file/690999/Children_in_Need_of_help_and_protection_Data_and_analysis.pdf.

7   Home Office, Serious Violence Strategy [policy paper] (9 April 2018), p. 29. Available at: https://assets.publishing.service.gov.uk/government/uploads/system/uploads/attachment_ data/file/698009/serious-violence-strategy.pdf.

8   Department for Education, Key Stage 4 Performance 2019 (Revised) [national statistics] (7 September 2020). National Tables: Table 2. Available at: https://www.gov.uk/government/ statistics/key-stage-4-performance-2019-revised.

up almost half the prison population[9] and it is estimated that each one will go on to cost £370,000 in extra education, health, welfare and criminal justice spending.[10]

Vulnerable children quite simply become even more vulnerable when they have been excluded from school. The problem is passed on but, inevitably, someone, somewhere must pick up the pieces – if that is even possible. As a profession, we must not see challenging behaviour as someone else's problem. Taking a relational approach will help to stem the tide of unnecessarily giving up on the children who need us most.

Try this

- If you are a school leader, make a link with your local PRU, AP or SEMH special school. Arrange for your staff to do visits and see how these specialist settings work with the most challenging children. There may also be an opportunity for specialist staff to deliver some training at your school. Arranging visits might be logistically challenging but will be worth it if you are genuine about changing your approach and committing to working with children who are at risk of being excluded.

- If you are a head teacher or principal, consider recruiting senior leaders who have experience in AP. They will bring with them a wealth of knowledge and expertise in relational practice and will be a real asset to your team. There are leaders out there who have been through specialist training in alternative settings and are looking to return to mainstream as senior leaders.[11] They will be experts and add real value to your leadership team.

---

9   Kim Williams, Vea Papadopoulou and Natalie Booth, *Prisoners' Childhood and Family Backgrounds: Results from the Surveying Prisoner Crime Reduction (SPCR) Longitudinal Cohort Study of Prisoners*. Ministry of Justice Research Series 4/12 (March 2012), p. ii. Available at: https://assets.publishing.service.gov.uk/government/uploads/system/uploads/attachment_data/file/278837/prisoners-childhood-family-backgrounds.pdf.

10 Gill, Quilter-Pinner and Swift, *Making the Difference*, p. 22.

11 For example, The Difference is a leadership development programme that takes aspirant leaders from mainstream schools and immerses them in AP for two years, with the intention of them returning to mainstream as senior leaders: https://www.the-difference.com/.

> If you are a teacher or a member of support staff, ask your head teacher if you can visit a PRU, AP or SEMH school as part of your CPD. A full day (or more if you can wangle it) will give you a great insight into the work of specialists. You may even decide that you want to go and work there (I did). Spending time in one of these settings is far more powerful than going on a behaviour course led by someone who does not work in schools, let alone challenging ones.

If we are serious about making a culture change and moving away from a reliance on exclusions, then dispelling myths and looking through a different lens is crucial. It needs to begin with teacher training and continue throughout teachers' careers. Encouragingly, the Department for Education's *Early Career Framework* recognises the importance of children developing intrinsic motivation, related to their identity and values and also recognising the importance of relationships, stating that:

> Building effective relationships is easier when pupils believe that their feelings will be considered and understood.[12]

Therefore, it is vital that we do not lose sight of relationships and undermine them by leaping to exclusions.

Withdrawal and non-attendance

Exclusion can happen in other guises. Self-exclusion can be an unintended consequence of zero-tolerance systems. Children might not attend due to a lack of acceptance and heightened anxiety, rather than because a formal exclusion has been issued by the school. They therefore do not appear on the school's statistics as an exclusion; they are an 'attendance problem'. Thousands of pupils struggle with confidence, self-esteem and anxiety at school. Without a concerted effort from

---

12 Department for Education, *Early Career Framework*. Ref: DFE-00015-2019 (January 2019), p. 22. Available at: https://assets.publishing.service.gov.uk/government/uploads/system/uploads/attachment_data/file/913646/Early-Career_Framework.pdf.

schools, these pupils are essentially excluded. They are often ignored because they do not conform to school norms or have the confidence to engage.

Some parents will formally withdraw their children from school and elect to educate them at home. This is a totally legal and acceptable option, but often happens for the wrong reasons. For many home-educated children, school would be a much better place for them – if they felt accepted and supported. In the 2018/19 academic year, it was estimated that at any one point almost 65,000 children were being educated at home, according to the responding local education authorities (LEAs), and this was thought to be increasing by an average of 20% a year.[13] Many of these children's parents had been 'encouraged' by the school to elect to home-educate. I have seen letters issued to parents by schools that were pre-written on their behalf and only required their signature to validate a move to home education. Parents, without the will or ability to protest, will often agree with the school and off-roll their children. This means they no longer receive those phone calls from school informing them of behaviour incidents or exclusions. They may feel a sense of short-term relief because their child is no longer having constant problems in school; however, they are left with the legal responsibility to educate them at home. This burden is often too great, and the children will reappear in the school system elsewhere – often at a more understanding and empathetic school where a greater effort is made to meet their needs and make them feel welcome. Therefore, the compassionate, welcoming and inclusive schools cater to a disproportionate number of complex and vulnerable children. The cycle just repeats itself over and over again. Too often these children can fall through the cracks at numerous schools before ultimately ending up in AP where they eventually thrive.

In 2018/19 over 771,000 pupils were persistently absent from school (missing more than 10% of their sessions).[14] Over 60,000 pupils missed more than 50% of their school year in 2018/19.[15] Of these, significant numbers were children with special

---

13 Association of Directors of Children's Services, *Elective Home Education Survey 2019* (November 2019), p. 1. Available at: https://adcs.org.uk/assets/documentation/ADCS_ Elective_Home_Education_Survey_Analysis_FINAL.pdf.
14 Department for Education, Pupil Absence in Schools in England: 2018 to 2019, National and Local Authority Tables [national statistics] (26 March 2020). Table 1.2: pupil enrolments that are persistent absentees – state-funded primary, secondary and special schools. Available at: https://www.gov.uk/government/statistics/pupil-absence-in-schools-in-england-2018-to-2019.
15 Department for Education, Pupil Absence in Schools in England. Table 3.2: percentage of enrolments by their overall absence rates – state-funded primary, secondary and special schools.

educational needs (SEN) and pupils on free school meals. This was not through formal exclusion but through 'choice'. Why are children choosing (or refusing) to attend and what can we do about it? School exclusion is therefore broader than the formalities of the behaviour policy; exclusion can be unofficial, with thousands of children not 'fitting in' or not being supported to attend. Many of these children harbour anxieties that are not addressed and so they fall into a black hole of non-attendance.

As relational practitioners, we can help to reduce this unacceptable level of hidden exclusions. We can make it our priority to be accepting and welcoming – adapting to the needs of our pupils as best we can. Without acceptance, these numbers will keep rising as more and more children find it impossible to attend school. Again, we must stop trying to fit square pegs into round holes – we need holes of all shapes and sizes, so every peg has somewhere to fit.[16]

16 More information and support for children who are struggling to access school can be found at: https://www.teamsquarepeg.org/.

Conclusion: Creating a legacy

Experience is, for me, the highest authority. The touchstone of validity is my own experience.

Carl Rogers[1]

You will be remembered both for your own behaviour and for how you dealt with the behaviour of others. That will define your legacy and is within your power to control. Your personal journey to self-actualisation – to achieving your full potential and fulfilling your career needs – will involve thousands of interactions and connections. Each one of those will influence how people perceive you and contribute to you being able to show your true self. Taking a relational approach relies heavily on allowing yourself to be authentic and creating the right environment in which to do so.

Learn from those you admire

You likely know, or have met, colleagues who inspire and motivate you. You will have seen fellow professionals who are able to create magic in their classrooms, on the sports pitches, in the science labs and in the corridors with the children. Many of these will have the most challenging pupils in the school wrapped around their little finger and eating out of the palm of their hand. When you see them, you wonder how they do it and what makes them so talented.

What you shouldn't forget is that they have probably been developing their relational skills for many years – there is invisible work at play here. The real experts have great relationships that have been developed over time and a commitment to making connections. These teachers and leaders are like icebergs: you can only see the tip. Under the surface is a disproportionately large, hard-fought relational

---

1   Rogers, *On Becoming a Person*, p. 23.

foundation – you cannot see it, but it is there. You will not become an expert over-night, and the skills and techniques need to be practised and rehearsed.

You will need to watch and learn from those you admire and those who have gen-uine experience. Unfortunately, you will also see 'professionals' who use fear and anxiety as a tool for compliance. You will be aware of adults who are happy to ridicule children, to belittle and humiliate them. However, without the use of sanc-tions and aggression these teachers are essentially useless. Steer clear of them in the staffroom as they will drain the lifeblood from you.

You must take every opportunity you can to learn from the wise. Wisdom is more than experience, skills and knowledge. Wisdom, in a relational sense, comes with qualities such as compassion and benevolence. Wisdom also comes with years of learning and exposure to the challenges faced in all schools, every day. Learning from those genuinely wise colleagues will contribute hugely to the development of your thinking and values. Think about who you are learning from – have they done it themselves and are they 'qualified' to advise and guide you? Can their 'expertise' be trusted?

Vulnerability is a virtue

You may often feel professionally and emotionally vulnerable when embarking on restorative practice. This can come when you feel exposed to situations that challenge you, or when your relationships are strained by differences in values. Vulnerability is something that you must accept. Without vulnerability you will develop arrogance. We are all vulnerable, and accepting this is not a weakness but a strength. It allows you to develop genuine empathy and to embrace your own development. Think about those colleagues you admire most – they too will be vulnerable in many ways but probably just hide it well.

I was lucky to be mentored and supported, throughout my career, by many leaders and colleagues who I respect for their wisdom – you need to find your counsel, as I still need mine. Align yourself with colleagues who share your values and do not allow yourself to be professionally corrupted by systems and processes that you oppose. If you are unable to influence change, and feel completely stifled, then you really do need to consider working somewhere where you can be happy and fulfilled. However, your fulfilment will not come overnight, and your own resilience will play a part in creating a legacy of which you can be proud.

Understanding needs

It would be remiss of us not to refer to Maslow's hierarchy of needs and its importance for understanding the journey of the children in our care.[2] Maslow's hierarchy allows us to understand the importance of providing what our pupils need. Their journey to self-fulfilment cannot happen without the foundations of basic physiological needs and safety being met. If children are not safe, fed, rested, and so on, then they will not thrive in a school environment; they will not make the important social connections they need, and self-esteem will be a distant goal. After establishing our basic physiological and safety needs, we move to the relational phase of friendship, intimacy and love – with that important sense of connection. Following this we unlock self-esteem, respect and recognition.

Maslow's famous pyramid (see page 132) can be used to plot your own career journey to self-actualisation.[3] It allows you to frame your professional journey to personal fulfilment – and therefore the basis of your legacy. Start with working in the right school, with people with whom you can connect. From there you grow your self-esteem and status, gaining recognition for the work you do. Then you can be the best that you can be – self-actualisation. This is the legacy phase – becoming who we want to be, giving our best and making a difference to the lives of others. Are you creating your own opportunities for self-actualisation? How is your past, and the present, shaping your future?

---

2   Abraham H. Maslow, A Theory of Human Motivation, *Psychological Review*, 50(4) (1943): 370–396. Available at: https://archive.org/details/MaslowA.H.1943. ATheoryOfHumanMotivation.PsychologicalReview504370-396./mode/2up.
3   Saul McLeod, Maslow's Hierarchy of Needs, *Simply Psychology* [blog] (20 March 2020). Available at: https://www.simplypsychology.org/maslow.html.

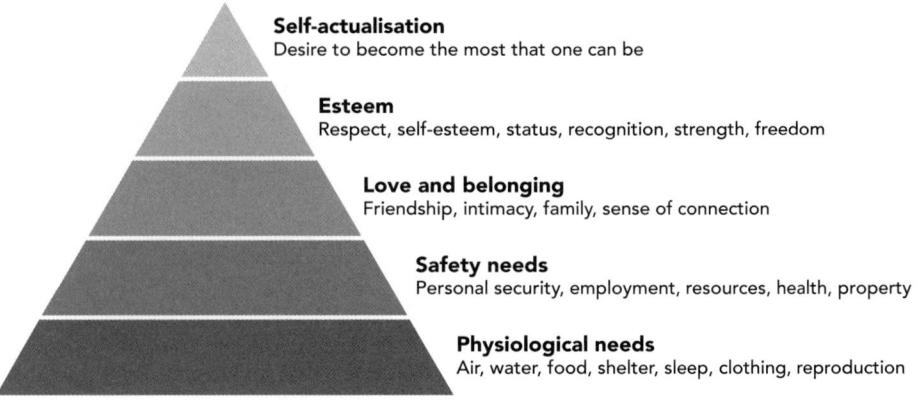

These are questions to consider in relation to your own behaviour. As you grow in experience, you will gain the confidence to trust your own judgements – either as a leader or a teacher. You will reduce your reliance on others to tell you what to do or guide you in a particular direction. As you become your true self, you should be aligning yourself with colleagues you trust, in a school whose values you share. Be reflective, always considering what people think of you, and also be mindful of your influence on others. After interacting with someone, take a reflective look at how you might have been perceived by them. Ask yourself how you would have felt if you had been on the receiving end of that interaction. Think carefully about how you make people feel and whether that aligns with your values.

How will you be remembered?

Many people remember their favourite teachers, but we also remember those we did not like or respect. Adults who are mean or nasty to children create memories that stick with them – perhaps some of your own teachers bring up long-lasting, negative connotations for you. It is the same with colleagues or leaders for whom we may have worked. I remember my own maths teacher. He would give us regular tests of our times tables in class. If you were unable to answer, or got it wrong, he would bring you to the front of the room, make you touch your toes and then whack your backside with a metre ruler. Did this motivate me? No. Did this inspire me? No. Did I resent and dislike him? Yes. Do I now know my times tables? No. Do I want to be remembered like this man? Absolutely not.

This was the 1980s and acceptable behaviour for a teacher. This was discipline at the cost of physical harm and public humiliation. That teacher's legacy is as an egotistical bully. My dad thought he was a great teacher because we were all scared of him, and my dad associated strict discipline with success. His own education in the 1940s and 1950s was clearly dominated by mean teachers wielding the cane and children 'knowing their place'. Although the metre ruler has now been decommissioned as a sanction, these teachers do still exist and still use fear and humiliation to gain compliance (and what they falsely believe is respect), just without a physical weapon; they rely solely on their hostile personalities. I am confident that my dad would now think differently about this approach, having spent hundreds of hours debating school behaviour with me over the last twenty-five years. However, he does like to disagree with me just for the love of a good argument.[4]

Ego can be a positive thing. It can give us the confidence and enthusiasm to want to progress and do well. However, letting your ego get the better of you, and becoming self-important and conceitful, will damage your professional relationships. This lack of humility will define your legacy and will hijack your journey to self-actualisation.

Confidence is great; arrogance is not. Your desire to keep on learning and developing will build your confidence. We all have more to learn and sustaining a culture of personalised CPD will give you the belief you need to strengthen professional relationships and further your career. A refusal to change, learn or develop will reinforce and fuel your arrogance. Do you want to be perceived as confident or arrogant?

As you develop as a professional (either as a teacher or school leader), your relational style will have an impact on others. Relational leaders empower and trust – they are ethical and purposeful. Moral values drive and motivate relational practitioners in

---

4   However, even with his love of a good argument, he has provided me with the ultimate protective relationship throughout my life. Always there, always solid, always reliable, always available – the greatest example of unconditional positive regard and a protective relationship. I am so lucky to have had the love and support of both my parents – something I never take for granted. My mum, a retired teacher who honed her trade in the council estates of West Yorkshire, is the kindest person I know, and her influence on my professional practice is profound.

the classroom and in the leadership office. However, we all make mistakes, and it would be unrealistic to think otherwise. Mistakes need to be corrected humanely and not at the expense of relationships or anyone's mental well-being – this applies to both adults and children. We can support and challenge (the social discipline window, yet again) with an understanding that we all get things wrong sometimes. There is never an excuse to be unpleasant to either colleagues or children – that, in my view, is bullying.

Being relational takes massive amounts of resilience. We cannot forget the importance of this when dealing with behaviour. You will be tested and challenged. It will feel like everything has gone wrong. You will find yourself working with, or for, colleagues who you do not respect. You will be prevented from making the changes you deem necessary. You may also find yourself trapped on a roller coaster of personal stress management, where your resilience will be buffered by your own supportive relationships. Schools are great places for developing support networks, as all your colleagues are going through the same challenges. Use these networks to laugh and cry together. Some of my best friends are people with whom I have worked in challenging circumstances. They understand it, have lived it, and have come through it – whatever 'it' may be.

When considering how you wish to be remembered, think about the following:

- Your relationships with pupils.

- Your relationships with staff.

- Your relationships with parents.

- Your relationships with leaders.

- Your relationships with governors.

Every one of these relationships counts and contributes to your legacy. If just one of these fails, then you risk damaging your legacy.

A few good friends and I were sitting outside a bar[5] in Barnsley – the town where the school in which we had worked together for many years had been.[6] (It has since been knocked down and replaced by houses – the school, not the bar.) As we sat

---

5 The Jolly Tap on the Arcade, a great place to go for a drink if ever you are in Barnsley.
6 The Kingstone School, a great school where I forged lifelong friendships.

drinking our lovely Yorkshire ale,[7] we were constantly interrupted by ex-pupils who we all knew from years of teaching in that town. Now adults, they still recognised us and stopped to talk. We were laughing and joking and they were recalling stories from our lessons, school musicals, school trips and residentials. They could remember specific lessons and even detailed interactions and conversations that took place nearly twenty years ago. We laughed together about past colleagues and about their own school friends, who we could all remember.

We also gracefully took the compliments about how much they loved being taught by us. They were open and honest about the respect they had for us and how the relationships they had forged with us were what they remembered most fondly about their time in education. They also told us the horror stories. They recounted tales of teachers who had treated them badly, who did not understand them and were generally rather horrible. It was clear that these now grown-up ex-pupils – and we met quite a few of them over the course of the evening – remembered vividly how their teachers had made them feel. In some cases, those feelings were still raw after all those years, and we could sense that they still carried a strong and lasting resentment of the way in which they had been treated.

The discussions we had that evening were legacy conversations. We had been judged over years of teaching hundreds of children and this was our data – it was action research. Although the sample was small, the results were consistent, and we enjoyed the warmth they showed us that evening. This was our legacy in action. Remember, relational practitioners are genuine and should aspire to the following traits:

- Kindness.

- Vulnerability.

- Dignity.

- Courage.

- Integrity.

- Humility.

---

7   The beer was brewed in Barnsley by the Jolly Boys' Brewery and is highly recommended.

If we can find these qualities within ourselves and look to exhibit them every day, then we are well on the way to creating a wonderful legacy.

Developing your own relational style will come with experience and, ultimately, wisdom. You may react and respond to the latest research and read the most acclaimed, 'innovative' new books, but there will never be a better endorsement of your legacy than the work you do in your school and the response you get from your pupils and colleagues. Your own validity comes with your legacy, and you are in control of that. You are the only one who can truly authenticate the way you are and the relationships you establish. Your legacy is therefore intrinsically created and validated by your relationships with others, especially the children you teach. Be your true self: that is the only validity you really need.

> I have come to feel that only one person can know whether what I am doing is honest, thorough, open and sound, or false and defensive and unsound, and I am that person.

> **Carl Rogers**[8]

Wise words indeed, Mr Rogers.

---

8   Rogers, *On Becoming a Person*, p. 23.

Bibliography

Association of Directors of Children's Services (2019) *Elective Home Education Survey 2019* (November). Available at: https://adcs.org.uk/assets/documentation/ADCS_Elective_Home_Education_Survey_Analysis_FINAL.pdf.

Bombèr, Louise and Daniel Hughes (2013) *Settling Troubled Pupils to Learn: Why Relationships Matter in School* (London: Worth Publishing).

Department for Education (2018) *Children in Need of Help and Protection: Data and Analysis*. Ref: DFE-00078-2018 (March). Available at: https://assets.publishing.service.gov.uk/government/uploads/system/uploads/attachment_data/file/690999/Children_in_Need_of_help_and_protection_Data_and_analysis.pdf.

Department for Education (2018) Permanent and Fixed-Period Exclusions in England: 2016 to 2017 [national statistics] (19 July). Available at: https://www.gov.uk/government/statistics/permanent-and-fixed-period-exclusions-in-england-2016-to-2017.

Department for Education (2018) Revised GCSE and Equivalent Results in England: 2016 to 2017 [national statistics] (25 January). Available at: https://www.gov.uk/government/statistics/revised-gcse-and-equivalent-results-in-england-2016-to-2017.

Department for Education (2018) Schools, Pupils and Their Characteristics: January 2018 [national statistics] (28 June). Available at: https://www.gov.uk/government/statistics/schools-pupils-and-their-characteristics-january-2018.

Department for Education (2019) *Early Career Framework*. Ref: DFE-00015-2019 (January). Available at: https://assets.publishing.service.gov.uk/government/uploads/system/uploads/attachment_data/file/913646/Early-Career_Framework.pdf.

Department for Education (2020) Key Stage 4 Performance 2019 (Revised) [national statistics] (7 September). National Tables: Table 2. Available at: https://www.gov.uk/government/statistics/key-stage-4-performance-2019-revised.

Department for Education (2020) Pupil Absence in Schools in England: 2018 to 2019, National and Local Authority Tables [national statistics] (26 March). Available at: https://www.gov.uk/government/statistics/pupil-absence-in-schools-in-england-2018-to-2019.

Department for Education and Department of Health (2015) *Special Educational Needs and Disability Code of Practice: 0 to 25 Years: Statutory Guidance for Organisations Which Work with and Support Children and Young People Who Have Special Educational Needs or Disabilities*. Ref: DFE-00205-2013 (January). Available at: https://assets.publishing.

service.gov.uk/government/uploads/system/uploads/attachment_data/file/398815/SEND_Code_of_Practice_January_2015.pdf.

Finnis, Mark (2021) *Independent Thinking on Restorative Practice: Building Relationships, Improving Behaviour and Creating Stronger Communities* (Carmarthen: Independent Thinking Press).

George, Martin (2019) Exclusive: Data Reveals Poor Pupils' Xmas Jumper Shame, *TES* (31 May). Available at: https://www.tes.com/news/exclusive-data-reveals-poor-pupils-xmas-jumper-shame.

Gill, Kiran, with Harry Quilter-Pinner and Danny Swift (2017) *Making the Difference: Breaking the Link between School Exclusion and Social Exclusion* (London: Institute for Public Policy Research). Available at: https://www.ippr.org/files/2017-10/making-the-difference-report-october-2017.pdf.

Ginott, Haim G. (1972) *Teacher and Child: A Book for Parents and Teachers* (New York: Macmillan).

Glaser, Daniel (1969) *The Effectiveness of a Prison and Parole System* (Indianapolis, IN: Bobbs-Merrill).

Golding, Kim S. (2015) Connection Before Correction: Supporting Parents to Meet the Challenges of Parenting Children who Have Been Traumatised within Their Early Parenting Environments, *Children Australia*, 40(2): 152–159.

Goulston, Mark (2008) *Post-Traumatic Stress Disorder for Dummies* (Hoboken, NJ: Wiley).

GriffinOT (2019) Sensory Integration Theory vs Sensory Processing Disorder What's the Difference? (27 December). Available at: https://www.griffinot.com/sensory-integration-sensory-processing/.

Hall, Karyn (2017) The Importance of Kindness, *Psychology Today* (4 December). Available at: https://www.psychologytoday.com/gb/blog/pieces-mind/201712/the-importance-kindness.

Halliday, Josh (2018) 'We Batter Them with Kindness': Schools That Reject Super-Strict Values, *The Guardian* (27 February). Available at: https://www.theguardian.com/education/2018/feb/27/schools-discipline-unconditional-positive-regard.

Hilton, James (1934) *Goodbye, Mr Chips* (London: Hodder & Stoughton).

Home Office (2018) *Serious Violence Strategy* [policy paper] (9 April). Available at: https://assets.publishing.service.gov.uk/government/uploads/system/uploads/attachment_data/file/698009/serious-violence-strategy.pdf.

Kinosian, Janet (2009) Q&A with the Late Coretta Scott King, *Huffington Post* [blog] (23 June). Available at: https://www.huffpost.com/entry/qa-with-the-late-coretta_b_94899.

Kohn, Alfie (1993) *Punished by Rewards: The Trouble with Gold Stars, Incentive Plans, A's, Praise, and Other Bribes* (Boston, MA: Houghton Mifflin Company).

McLeod, Saul (2014) Carl Rogers, *Simply Psychology* [blog] (5 February). Available at: https://www.simplypsychology.org/carl-rogers.html.

McLeod, Saul (2017) Bowlby's Attachment Theory, *Simply Psychology* [blog] (5 February). Available at: https://www.simplypsychology.org/bowlby.html.

McLeod, Saul (2020) Maslow's Hierarchy of Needs, *Simply Psychology* [blog] (20 March). Available at: https://www.simplypsychology.org/maslow.html.

Maslow, Abraham H. (1943) A Theory of Human Motivation, *Psychological Review*, 50(4): 370–396. Available at: https://archive.org/details/MaslowA.H.1943. ATheoryOfHumanMotivation.PsychologicalReview504370-396./mode/2up.

Moore, David (2011) The circle of intimacy [video] (21 November). Available at: https://www.youtube.com/watch?v=0A-iTNk0Cj4.

National Scientific Council on the Developing Child (2014) *Excessive Stress Disrupts the Architecture of the Developing Brain.* Working Paper No. 3 (Cambridge, MA: Harvard University Center on the Developing Child). Available at: https://developingchild. harvard.edu/wp-content/uploads/2005/05/Stress_Disrupts_Architecture_Developing_Brain-1.pdf.

Perry, Bruce D. (2001) The Neuroarcheology of Childhood Maltreatment: The Neurodevelopmental Costs of Adverse Childhood Events. In K. Franey, R. Geffner and R. Falconer (eds), *The Cost of Maltreatment: Who Pays? We All Do* (San Diego, CA: Family Violence and Sexual Assault Institute), pp. 15–37. Available at: https://divisionsbc.ca/ sites/default/files/Divisions/Nanaimo/Neuroarcheology_2001_web.pdf.

Perry, Bruce D. and Christine L. Dobson (2013) The Neurosequential Model of Therapeutics. In Julian D. Ford and Christine A. Courtois (eds), *Treating Complex Traumatic Stress Disorders in Children and Adolescents, Scientific Foundations and Therapeutic Models* (New York: The Guilford Press), pp. 249–260.

Perry, Philippa (2019) *The Book You Wish Your Parents Had Read (and Your Children Will Be Glad That You Did)* (London: Penguin Life).

Porges, Stephen W. (2011) *The Polyvagal Theory: Neurophysiological Foundations of Emotions, Attachment, Communication, and Self-Regulation* (New York: W. W. Norton).

Renick, Christie (2018) Inside the Bruce Perry Show, *The Imprint* (23 May). Available at: https://imprintnews.org/news-2/inside-the-bruce-perry-show/30963.

Rhodes, Igraine and Michelle Long (2019) *Improving Behaviour in Schools: Guidance Report* (London: Education Endowment Foundation). Available at: https://educationendowmentfoundation.org.uk/tools/guidance-reports/improving-behaviour-in-schools/.

Roberts, Hywel (2012) *Oops! Helping Children Learn Accidentally* (Carmarthen: Independent Thinking Press).

Rogers, Bill (2015) *Classroom Behaviour: A Practical Guide to Effective Teaching, Behaviour Management and Colleague Support*, 4th edn (London: SAGE Publications).

Rogers, Carl R. (1961) *On Becoming a Person: A Therapist's View of Psychotherapy* (Boston, MA, and New York: Houghton Mifflin Company).

Schilling, Elizabeth A., Robert H. Aseltine Jr and Susan Gore (2007) Adverse Childhood Experiences and Mental Health in Young Adults: A Longitudinal Survey, *BMC Public Health*, 7(30). Available at: https://link.springer.com/article/10.1186/1471-2458-7-30.

Siegel, Daniel J. (2002) *The Developing Mind: How Relationships and the Brain Interact to Shape Who We Are* (New York: Guilford Press).

Wachtel, Ted and Paul McCold (2008) Restorative Justice in Everyday Life. In Heather Strang and John Braithwaite (eds), *Restorative Justice and Civil Society* (Cambridge: Cambridge University Press), pp. 114–129.

Whitaker, Dave (2015) The Values Seesaw. In Ian Gilbert (ed.), *There is Another Way: The Second Big Book of Independent Thinking* (Carmarthen: Independent Thinking Press), pp. 49–54.

Wilde, Oscar (1885) The Relation of Dress to Art: A Note in Black and White on Mr. Whistler's Lecture, *Pall Mall Gazette* (28 February). In Robert Ross (ed.) *Miscellanies by Oscar Wilde*, Project Gutenberg ebook edn. Available at: http://www.gutenberg.org/files/14062/14062-h/14062-h.htm.

Williams, Kim, Vea Papadopoulou and Natalie Booth (2012) *Prisoners' Childhood and Family Backgrounds: Results from the Surveying Prisoner Crime Reduction (SPCR) Longitudinal Cohort Study of Prisoners*. Ministry of Justice Research Series 4/12 (March). Available at: https://assets.publishing.service.gov.uk/government/uploads/system/uploads/attachment_data/file/278837/prisoners-childhood-family-backgrounds.pdf.

Wood, Fiona (2015) *Six Impossible Things* (New York and Boston: Little, Brown and Company).

Wood, Phil (2019) Dave Whitaker – Unconditional Positive Regard: Developing High-Quality Alternative Provision, *Management in Education*, 33(3): 147–149.

Wood, Phil (2019) Rethinking Time in the Workload Debate, *Management in Education*, 33(2): 86–90.